UP
AGAINST
THE BRASS

by ANDY STAPP

SIMON AND SCHUSTER
New York

FIRST PRINTING

SBN 671-20572-2 CLOTH
SBN 671-20775-X PAPER
LIBRARY OF CONGRESS CATALOG CARD NUMBER: 71-107266
DESIGNED BY IRVING PERKINS
MANUFACTURED IN THE UNITED STATES OF AMERICA

This book is dedicated to
TERRY KLUG, BILL BRAKEFIELD, JEFFREY RUSSELL
and all the other ASU *members*
in stockades and brigs around the world.

I wish to express my deep thanks to Libby Copeland, without whose aid this book would never have been written.

PART ONE

CHAPTER I
It was hot. Hot the way Oklahoma around Fort Sill in midsummer is hot. Dry, dusty, with a bright sun scorching everything to brown—a burning, blistering, brutal sun that no one stands out in for long, except soldiers.

Sixty of us had been drawn up in four ranks as an honor guard to watch officers award each other medals. I stood in the front and could hear the occasional movements of the others behind me.

We had been standing for thirty minutes. Sweat was running down my face and streaking through my uniform. My muscles ached. My rifle cut a painful notch in my shoulder. Already one man had collapsed with a clatter of falling rifle and helmet, done in by one-hundred-and-five-degree heat.

In front of us, looking small against the vast flat expanse of dry field that stretched endlessly, stood a row of officers who periodically stepped forward one by one to stand at attention in front of a captain with a soft-white, college-professor face. In the approved military monotone the captain recited the heroic acts committed by these officers in Vietnam.

"Captain Simpson, forty-two successful missions, the Air Medal."

Next to the college-professor captain stood two sergeants. They wore white gloves and had tiny carbines slung on their shoulders. They saluted Captain Simpson when he came forward to receive his award.

"Lieutenant Johnson, for meritorious service in the Republic of Vietnam, June 1965 to June 1966, the Silver Star."

Another officer came forward, the white-gloved sergeants saluted, the ceremony was repeated. Then the awarding captain began to read again.

In the ranks, hot, aching and miserable, each of us studied the remaining row of officers and the sheets of paper in the captain's hand and tried to imagine an end to our misery.

Repeatedly now I envisioned myself throwing down my rifle and saying, "Fuck you and this whole goddam mess, what am I doing in an Army that is killing people ten thousand miles away in their own country in a war that I know is rotten and that I hate enough to get arrested demonstrating against?"

"Captain, then Lieutenant, Whittier, guiding his K-9 dog with complete disregard for his own safety, chased the Vietcong into a bunker. Captain, then Lieutenant, Whittier hurled a grenade into the bunker. The Vietcong threw the grenade out of the bunker, killing Captain Whittier's dog and wounding Captain Whittier."

"Too bad it wasn't the other way around," said a voice from behind me.

There were snorts of laughter in the ranks but they were inaudible to the officers standing thirty feet away.

I smiled and my feelings of frustration lessened because I knew again even more surely that sooner or later I would succeed in enlisting the support of these guys against the

Army, against the officers and against the war. And that was what I had come into this Army for in the first place.

It was on a trip to Egypt in 1964 that I first came to question the Vietnam war. I had been raised in a comfortable Philadelphia suburb and the war had seemed far away and not too important. Even when I entered Penn State it had held little interest for me. I was an archaeology major, and in the spring of 1964 I went with an expedition from the college to Egypt to study the magnificent sculptures at Abu Simbel, which were going to be inundated by the Aswan Dam.

I went to Egypt to learn about ancient history. Instead I learned about modern history, about the Egyptians' struggle against the British and about the horrible legacy left by the British, a legacy of squalor and ignorance and disease.

What I saw and heard made me realize that British colonialism was not typified by white suits and gin and sodas and stiff upper lips. It really meant brutal, systematic oppression of whole peoples, slavery, drudgery and death.

English troops landed in Egypt in 1882. They had been sent by London to crush a nationalist rebellion against the Khedive of Cairo, a pro-British puppet, and the troops remained for sixty-five years. When World War II ended there was a wave of anti-imperialist sentiment and the English were forced to withdraw their troops. In 1952 the thoroughly corrupt King Farouk was overthrown by a revolution that openly proclaimed itself against colonialism, imperialism and monopolies. The Egyptian Republic, established in 1953, recognized for the first time in Egypt's six-thousand-year history that the people had the right to own the land they tilled. The Agrarian Law, aimed at destroying the power of a tiny clique of great landowners, limited the amount of land any single individual could hold.

With the departure of the British came improvements. I saw bright new buildings going up in Cairo. I watched the construction of new housing projects. I witnessed the completion of the Aswan Dam, a glittering testament to a genuine effort to improve conditions. But for many Egyptians the improvements came far too late. The viciousness of colonialism had left them hopelessly unable to cope with the demands of modern civilization.

I later learned that the United States Army indoctrinated its troops with a view vastly different from what colonialism had meant to subjugated peoples. I'll quote from an Army handbook titled *Democracy vs. Communism,* published by the Institute of Fiscal and Political Education and widely used by the Army for indoctrination purposes: "In time, the European governing groups in these empires put an end to tribal warfare among the native peoples. European merchants and traders developed local industry. Railroads and canals were built. Public health and sanitation were improved, schools and churches were established and missionaries brought hope and new religious ideas as well as medical care to millions of people."

It would be hard to convince the suffering masses in Egypt that this glib rationale held any truth whatsoever, and it is to honor them that the Egyptians have left Shepheard's Hotel standing.

Shepheard's was an English hotel that had been blown half apart by grenades hurled by guerrilla fighters whose intense hatred of what the British had done to them, their families and their country made them willing to die rather than let England continue her rule. And after the British left, the Egyptians kept Shepheard's Hotel as a reminder of what England had done.

I returned to Penn State in July 1964 firmly convinced that no nation had the right to impose its will on another. Was that what was happening in Vietnam? Was what Hubert Humphrey described as a "great adventure" really a shabby cover-up for something else? I had to know.

The following month, August 1964, the Students for a Democratic Society at Penn State distributed a leaflet on which was a picture millions of Americans have since seen. The picture showed a National Liberation Front (NLF) prisoner being dragged behind a U.S. Army half-track. Seeing the United States employ this kind of torture was like being punched in the guts. I still remember the picture's caption: "The long slow slide into barbarism is quickening."

I began studying the background and the events of the war, and the more I read the more I discovered what a hypocritical role the government was playing. They placed puppets in power and preached democracy. They killed and said they abhorred violence. They burned and bombed and called it progress.

My whole world changed. How could I stay on a serene campus and prepare for a comfortable life while America waged a war that killed innocent people?

I did not belong to SDS or any other group at this time, but when I heard of a demonstration in Washington called by the Assembly of Unrepresented People I went.

I hitchhiked to Washington on Hiroshima Day, August 6, 1965, and for the first time witnessed what the authorities do to those who try to oppose them.

I was among a group that staged a sit-in at the gates of the White House. We were angry about the war and wanted to say so, and sitting there seemed a way to do it. We were causing some inconvenience and some commotion, probably, but we weren't endangering anyone, unless airing opposition ideas is a danger to the ruling powers. The Government's response was to send several hundred policemen to arrest us. They threw us into paddy wagons and tossed tear gas into the paddy wagons while we were locked inside. The police were very patriotic. I thought I would choke to death.

We were bailed out of jail almost immediately by some people whom I'd never heard of before and haven't heard of since but who earned our gratitude that day. Twenty-four hours later we marched on the Capitol.

The police warned us not to get closer than three blocks from the Capitol, but we kept marching. Police jumped in and clubbed us down. I was beaten unconscious. A friend of mine took pictures of the clubbings. One showed a policeman standing on my neck. Three hundred and sixty-one of us were herded into buses and paddy wagons and I remember seeing a lot of blood. Blood was everywhere, on the ceiling and the wall and the seats, but mostly on people who had just wanted to show their displeasure with a war they had voted against nine months before.

My second stay in jail was different from the first. I refused to give my name or cooperate in any way until I was allowed to see an attorney. When I refused to let them take my fingerprints a policeman pulled out a steel whip and laced me across the arms until they went involuntarily limp. Then they fingerprinted me.

I continued to refuse to give my name, so they put me in a cell apart from the other prisoners. At one point four guards grabbed me and walked me into a wall. It knocked me unconscious and broke one of my teeth. Finally they put me back in with the rest.

It was during this time in jail that I first read genuine antiwar literature. One of the arrested demonstrators wore heavy boots. Although the police had taken anything remotely resembling literature from everyone else, they hadn't discovered what he had hidden in his boots. He pulled it out and passed it around.

Where before I had seen the evils of English colonialism, now I began to get a glimmer of the nature of finance capitalism and its demand for foreign markets and raw materials at the expense of the world's people.

I was kept in jail because I refused to go before a judge without a lawyer. I said that I wanted a lawyer, that I had a right to a lawyer and that if they took me to court without one I would holler and struggle in every way I could to disrupt the proceedings.

"You do that and you'll get a year in jail," a sergeant told me.

"Take me in there without a lawyer and you'll see what I'll do."

They didn't take me. Finally they produced an attorney. I was found guilty of disorderly conduct and fined twenty-five dollars. I had been in jail eleven days.

I returned to Penn State and along with several other students became active in antiwar activity. I was elected president of the group. Our intention was to encourage draft resistance among students. Earlier that year Congress had passed a law making draft-card burning illegal and punishable by five years in prison. We felt the best way to destroy this kind of police-state law was for everyone to violate it. We felt that if enough people could be persuaded to disobey the law it would become a dead letter. On October 16, 1965, at a street meeting on the Penn State campus, a number of us set fire to our draft cards. We burned them in a Nazi helmet.

But in spite of our efforts, massive draft resistance did not build up as we had hoped. Instead, some citizens seemed more outraged at draft-card burners than at a Government that burned women and children with napalm.

The war went on. The killing went on. I became increas-

ingly frustrated. I wanted to do something, I felt an obligation to do something to end the slaughter. But I seemed sty-
mied. We had the support of many Penn State students, but
most were afraid to risk prison by joining us. Our problem
was similar to what SDS experiences are today. Despite
claims to the contrary, a majority of college students seem
to be in sympathy with what SDS is trying to do. But they're
afraid "to put it all on the line," especially with law-and-
order advocates seeming to have carried the day. So it was
with us in 1965. We had support. We didn't have enough
people willing to take a big step—namely, to burn their
draft cards.

I reported for my induction physical in December 1965,
believing I could be more effective if I joined the Army and
organized from within. After all, it was the GIs who faced
the immediate prospect of death in Vietnam. And it was the
GIs who, if they refused to fight, could bring a sudden halt
to the war. I felt reasonably sure that Lyndon Johnson and
Dean Rusk weren't so convinced of the justness of the war
that they would fight it themselves.

Months went by and I wasn't called. In April 1966 I went
to the draft board and asked why.

"We can't take you. You don't have a draft card."

"Get me one. I want to serve the country the best way I
know how."

I was drafted into the Army on Friday, May 13, 1966. It
was to be an unlucky day for them, not me. I became US
52666589.

It was, I imagine, a typical swearing-in ceremony. The
lieutenant told us that if anyone went AWOL he would
probably be shot, because there was a war on. Apparently
quite a few before us had already gone over the hill, but I

didn't think the lieutenant's absurd threat was going to deter many people.

It didn't. As our train pulled out for the long, hot ride to South Carolina, we saw one of the guys who had been inducted with us. He was on the train going the other way, north to New York. He was AWOL.

CHAPTER II   Even in May 1966, during the start of basic training at Fort Jackson, South Carolina, my thoughts centered solely on how I was going to organize effective dissent against the war in Vietnam.

I was confident. Perhaps too confident. But I had had success recruiting at Penn State and I thought I had an understanding of the real issues and could present them clearly and convincingly. It was probably fortunate that I did have confidence. Perhaps if I had thought about the long odds I faced, I would have become discouraged. No one was backing me. No one had given advice on how I should begin. No one was even committed to working with me.

But *I* was committed. I was going to take on the United States Army, and if it meant the stockade, so be it.

Most Army bases are located in warm climates. Fort Jackson is one of the largest and stands near Columbia, South Carolina's capital. Fort Jackson is tens of thousands of acres of sand and scrub-pine country.

When the train arrived we were lined up alongside it, then marched in ragged ranks from the railroad station to the reception center. On the front of the building was a red, white and blue sign that proclaimed: WELCOME TO THE UNITED STATES ARMY.

Once inside, we sat down and waited. Then a big man, a first sergeant, red-faced and barrel-chested, stood up on a slightly elevated stage and took charge.

There must have been a thousand of us in the room. It was hot and stuffy and we could smell each other. There was a lot of foot-shuffling and the sergeant said, "Shut up."

The faces of the men were strained. On the train down they had been loud, too loud, their brittle bravado masking a host of fears.

"Do as you're told and you'll get along fine," the sergeant told us. "Be a wise guy and we'll cut you in half."

I accomplished very little at Fort Jackson. Anyone who has gone through basic training will understand why. Most of the men were simply too worn down by the physical demands of the sergeants to entertain ideas that might otherwise have challenged and stimulated. I knew there was no sense pushing it. After a long day in the South Carolina heat, any normal soldier wanted only to lie down on his bunk and sleep. I did manage to obtain from the base library three copies of Bob Taber's *The War of the Flea,* an account of the Cuban revolution written by a participant. Several GIs read it and discussed it.

Although the time was wrong for any positive action on my part, there was an anti-Army education that no words or literature could match. The arrogance of the officers—"Say 'sir' when you speak to me"—the regulation that forces a soldier to leap to his feet and call "Attention!" whenever an officer enters the barracks, the vast difference between the pay and the living quarters of the brass compared to that of the GI, the crudeness of the sergeants, the unnecessary work details, the rotten food—all these factors and more helped create an abiding dislike for the Army. I saw this and intended to use it to advantage. Nonetheless, when basic training ended and I was sent to Fort Sill, Oklahoma, I was not happy. I hadn't recruited a single dissenter. Thousands had died in Vietnam while I had gone on mindless marches.

Forty-five thousand men are stationed at Fort Sill, the nation's largest base for artillery and officer training. I arrived in July, a beastly hot, hundred-degree day that sapped the strength and killed the spirit. I was driven past comfortable, air-conditioned, Spanish-style officers' bungalows to the dreary barracks where enlisted men live.

Fort Sill has an interesting history. The Treaty of Medicine Lodge, of October 1867, reserved the land of Western Oklahoma for the Kiowas, Comanches and Apaches. The treaty's purpose was to force all Indians west of the Mississippi. One year later—1868—General Sheridan came to what is now Fort Sill and began a systematic extermination of the red man. Geronimo, the great Apache chief, the Indians' most eloquent and determined spokesman, was held captive at Fort Sill for years and died there in 1913.

Recruits aren't taught the history of Fort Sill. Instead they learn how to bring mortar and artillery fire down on guerrilla emplacements, how to fire pistols and rifles and machine guns, how to rip a man from throat to crotch with a bayonet, how to bomb and strafe, how to handle napalm and antipersonnel bombs and how to chart the arc of trajectories so that people will be killed as efficiently as possible in as short a time as possible.

My plan to organize resistance against the Vietnam war had a number of things going for it, among them a course the officers at Fort Sill labeled "Character Guidance." Character Guidance taught us three things: Americans are citizens of the greatest country in the world; the enemies are "Chinks" and "gooks"; and, third, how to answer the instructor's questions.

"What does the soldier want?"

"To kill! To kill!"

"What are you?"

"Soldiers!"

"What are you, really?"

"Tigers!"

"What do you eat?"

"Raw meat!"

"What do you drink?"

"Red blood!"

"Whose blood?"

"Gooks' blood!"

I was among a few who refused to take part in this lesson in character guidance, though the class was so large I doubt if the instructor noticed. But, listening to the chant, I was reminded of something. It was a long time before I could pinpoint it—the cry of Franco's soldiers: "Long Live Death!"

Segregation is no longer officially practiced in the Army, but in fact black GIs are separated from whites through work assignments. Artillery training is an example. The heavy and dangerous work of loading and firing the big guns is invariably handled by blacks, while fire and direction control, surveying and clerical jobs are assigned to whites.

Some of the GIs at Fort Sill had gone through basic training with me at Fort Jackson. They had sensed how I felt about the war. Soon they were sure. I explained what I believed, what I planned to do, how they could help. Many were interested. A few agreed to join forces with me and actively oppose the war. But before that could be, every single one was shipped out to Germany or Vietnam. The only explanation I could think of seemed farfetched. I wasn't willing to accept it yet.

I soon found another ally—Jerry Sylvester, a former construction worker from New York City. Jerry had been an athlete, was tall and husky, good-natured, the live-and-let-live kind of guy who automatically dislikes the Army. Jerry was intelligent, too, and had a touch of the crusader in him. Sure, he said, he'd help me talk to the guys. He was going with a girl in New York and he didn't feel like risking his life just because officers said he should. And there wasn't anybody going to say Jerry Sylvester was a coward. His size, his participation in Golden Gloves, the very physical work he had done in civilian life, these and more told the world Jerry Sylvester was no coward.

The two of us conducted bull sessions each night after "lights-out." Within a week we had more than thirty GIs in the discussions, asking questions, trading ideas, beginning to think, maybe, that after all, what the war really was was a piece of shit, and why should they get down on all fours and roll in it?

Word of our late-night sessions got around. Among others, it got around to some of the Marine NCOs who were training at the Fort Sill Artillery School. It got around to Corporal John Clayton Holland.

Corporal John Clayton Holland was from Midnight, Mississippi, and he believed in the war. He also believed in the Marine Corps. He was going to be a lifer, a man who selflessly sacrifices his own life for the preservation of freedom. Corporal John Clayton Holland didn't like a pair of "Communists" like Jerry Sylvester and Andy Stapp bad-mouthing the Government.

The Army has strange customs. One of these was that Marine Corporal John Clayton Holland had absolute authority over Army Privates Sylvester and Stapp. First, he lifted our weekend passes. When he learned that we were perfectly happy with that arrangement, since we wanted to organize in the barracks, not party in town, he adopted a different tack: he ordered a special formation of our entire sixty-man section for 5 A.M., August 28, 1966. The formation took place on Fort Sill's baseball field, and after everyone had fallen into line, Corporal Holland ordered us to sit in the bleacher seats. For what seemed a long time he stood below us looking up, then he told Jerry and me to come out of the bleachers and stand in front of him.

"Staaaaaapp," he said in a slow southern drawl, "Ah'm givin' yew ohdahs tew dew tew hunderd exacizes of yewr own choice. Which exacize dew yew choose tew dew?"

He had the scene all worked out in his mind. In front of the other men he would humiliate this wise-assed kid from New York, or Philadelphia, or whatever northern city he was from. He would make this kid get down on his belly and sweat and strain and grunt while he, Marine Corporal John Clayton Holland of Midnight, Mississippi, stood over him and made clever remarks.

"Which dew yew choose, Staaaaaapp?"

He had misjudged the situation. Most of the soldiers in the bleachers were sympathetic to what Jerry and I had been saying. Those who weren't sympathetic were neutral. There had been no hostility toward us. Vietnam was a potential death sentence hanging over all our heads and no one felt much empathy with the views of someone so obviously on the side of those who passed the sentence. Also, nearly every man in the group was a draftee, dragged into an Army he would never have volunteered for, and that sort of soldier dislikes—no, hates—a lifer.

"Ah'll ask yew once moah, Staaaaaapp, which dew yew choose tew dew?"

"None."

"Let him alone, you bastard," someone called from the bleachers.

"Yew are goin' tew pay foah this, Staaaaaapp. Ah'm goin' tew—"

"You're going to hell, you son-of-a-bitch." This time I recognized the voice. It belonged to a GI who hadn't been overly impressed by our antiwar ideas.

Soon there were other voices coming from the bleachers. Angry voices. The men had been forced to rise before daybreak, they were tired and irritable; more important, they resented an Army code that gave a Marine corporal life-and-death authority over them. I thought that if Holland had any common sense he would drop the issue. But Midnight, Mississippi's finest was not one to back away from an issue.

"Sylvestah, which exacize—"

"Fuck you," Jerry said.

Corporal Holland looked up at the bleachers, then at Jerry and me. "Yew may go," he said, "but this is not the end of the mattah."

That night a number of fellow GIs joined Jerry and me over beers. For us it was the celebration of a first, and admittedly modest, victory.

CHAPTER III   In September 1966, two weeks after the incident with John Clayton Holland on the baseball field, our entire barracks was broken up and scattered between bases from Europe to Vietnam. I was the only GI not transferred. Why? The only answer I could come up with was the same one I had rejected before. I couldn't believe it was true. I asked an NCO.

"Make a guess, you fucking red," he answered.

I later learned that months before I had been drafted, the Army had assembled a fairly complete dossier on my anti-war activities at Penn State.

For an instant I was flattered. The Army's afraid of me, I thought. Then I realized the truth and felt depressed. Since they were aware of my purpose they could easily counter any measures I might employ. I imagined that every time I formed a small corps of resistance the Army would render it impotent by merely signing some transfer papers.

To hell with it, I thought. There's got to be a way. You'll find it.

I wanted to find it soon. Despite assurances from General Westmoreland that the National Liberation Front would soon topple because their "attrition rate" was high, from Robert McNamara that there was "a light at the end of the tunnel," and from Lyndon Johnson, who was willing to do "anything" for peace, the toll of dead marched grimly upward.

Before Jerry Sylvester was transferred, the two of us were called to appear before a pair of Battalion S-2 officers, members of Military Intelligence, to answer questions about our political views. We were shepherded into the room together, introduced to a studious-looking lieutenant and a crew-cut captain. The captain did the talking.

"Where do you get your ideas? Books? What books do you read, Stapp?"

Bitter experience would teach me to answer nothing. But that was in the future. I said, "What I read is my business."

"Tough little shit, huh?" He turned to Jerry and asked if he had read any of my books. At first Jerry said he hadn't, and then, with the ghost of a smile, said, "Well, yes, I did read *The Thurber Carnival.*"

"Thurber?" the lieutenant said. "Thurber? Isn't he——?"

"I think he is," the captain said darkly.

The captain decided it was time to find out what I kept in my foot locker, so we followed him to the barracks. He ordered me to open the locker and I did. It was bulging with thirty-one books and periodicals.

The captain took them all. He said he would return them the next day. He even gave me a typewritten list of what he took. It was captioned: "Received from Private Andrew D. Stapp the following manuels [sic]."

One year and two courts-martial later I got them back.

After this incident the brass decided to keep a closer watch on me. I tried to ignore petty harassments such as the almost daily search of my foot locker. Now that my buddies had been shipped out, I had to start all over again finding soldiers who would listen to arguments against the war.

In October 1966 I was assigned to the First Officer Student Battery—not to train to be an officer, but to clean the quarters of the men who were being trained and to rake the leaves off the lawn outside the officers' club. Once I spray-painted the grass green because the Inspector General was coming to Fort Sill and the brass wanted it to look as though it had had a lot of nourishment. It was a case of the incompetent forcing the unwilling to do the unnecessary.

But my main job was at the post office. Since I lacked the security clearance needed to work inside on the mail, I worked outside weeding the gardens.

Then I got a break and a welcome but unexpected vacation. Each morning the sergeant read off our names and assigned us a job. Suddenly he stopped calling the name Stapp. I did hear him call for Andrews, who didn't answer, and I thought maybe Andrews was sick or AWOL. Not having an assignment, I went to the library and read.

On the morning of the fourth day the sergeant began getting worried about Andrews' continuing absence. Did any of us know where Andrews was? he wanted to know. He said he would have our hides if we were concealing information. By that time I realized that Andrews must be me (the clerk at the personnel office had switched my first and last names), but I didn't tell the sergeant. I just fell in line with the other GIs who were assigned to the post office.

"Who are you?" a post office sergeant asked when we arrived.

"Private Stapp," I said, "sent to work here."

"You must be the replacement for that son-of-a-bitch Andrews. He hasn't showed for three days. When we catch him it'll be for the stockade."

But they never caught him. And three weeks later I was transferred to the Second of the Second—the Second Howitzer Battalion, Second Artillery Brigade—a crack outfit at Fort Sill and the oldest artillery unit at the base.

When a GI enters a new unit he has to be cleared through various departments. One of these is S-2, Battalion Intelligence. I was sent to see Sergeant Ogletre, the S-2 NCO. Ogletre, an unlikely James Bond, was called "007" by the men. He gave me a quick clearance and sent me to Major Smith, the battalion executive officer.

This wasn't standard procedure, but I didn't realize it at the time. New recruits simply don't get greeted by battalion executive officers unless there's a reason. I later learned that Military Intelligence had sent in a special report on me and had requested that I be assigned a separate room. They had said I was a possible risk to national security.

But Major Smith's superior, the battalion colonel, refused to go along with Military Intelligence. He felt it wasn't proper for an enlisted man to have his own room, even in the interests of national security. Separate rooms were reserved for officers. Of course I wanted to be in the barracks, so I was pleased with his ruling.

I felt pretty isolated at first, though. I had never had trouble making friends before, but now the other men usually avoided me. One night I came into the barracks late and heard someone whisper, "It's Stapp." It threw me for a while. I wondered how they could dislike me; they didn't even know me yet. Later I found out that the brass had told them to keep away from me, that I was a Communist.

I was assigned to permanent latrine duty. I was the latrine guard, and it was not a very pleasant or interesting job. And it wasn't the kind of job they put a man on permanently— unless they were trying to tell him something.

In December 1966 one of the Spec Fives in the unit, John Quincy Adams (a direct descendant of the John Quincy Adams in history books) stopped and asked why I was on permanent latrine duty. I told him about how I had tried to organize war resistance and how my books had been taken away.

Adams was something of a freethinker and told two of his friends about me. They were Paul Gaedtke and Dick Wheaton. Both were Spec Fives, both were in fire direction control. In the days that followed they became my staunch allies.

At first they were cautious and reserved, but I welcomed their company and was grateful to have someone to talk with. Since Jerry Sylvester had been transferred (he was sent to Vietnam and I never heard from him again) I had been pretty much alone.

A Specialist Five, the rank Paul Gaedtke and Dick Wheaton held, is the highest rank an enlisted man usually makes during his two years in the Army. On occasion, however, a Spec Five does go to Officer Candidate School. That was what Wheaton and Gaedtke were hoping for, but because of our subsequent activities together, they never made it.

Paul Gaedtke was from Indiana. Before entering the Army he had never been away from home. He was from a working-class family, and the last job he had had was spray-painting cars in a garage. When he began coughing up blue phlegm he quit and enlisted. Gaedtke was sandy-haired and husky and handsome, an all-American-type regular guy, just what the Army was looking for. He liked a good drink and a good fight. He was hot-headed, fearless, a daredevil who would be invaluable in combat. The Army recognized these qualities and Gaedtke rose rapidly, going from E-1 to E-5 in a year. The Army sent him on secret missions to guard ammo trains and gave him the highest security clearance of any man in the battalion.

Dick Wheaton, though just as regular in appearance and

manner and background as Gaedtke, was a different type entirely. He was reserved and levelheaded. He never made up his mind in a hurry, but when he did, it stayed that way. Wheaton had an excellent mind and proved to be a first-rate public speaker. He was from Detroit and before joining the Army had been a successful musician. When I met him he was a trusted stockade guard, possessed of an enormous inner strength that would later be summoned to withstand a hell of a lot of pressure.

Neither Gaedtke nor Wheaton had ever come up against radical ideas before. They had never seen a draft card burned, a student demonstrate. They were not eager to go to Vietnam, but it had never occurred to them to refuse. And, like anyone else, they welcomed advancement because it meant easier work and higher pay.

Gaedtke and Wheaton had only one complaint against the Army—the brass.

"They treat people like animals," Gaedtke said. "When I make officer I'll treat them like human beings."

"Like hell," I said. "When you get to be an officer you'll change. You'll have a different outlook. It's like when you get money. Then you're more interested in preserving and increasing what you have than in working to make sure others have enough. Sure, when you make officer you'll try to stay the same. But the brass won't let you. They'll make you carry out orders that push the men under you to impossible tasks. The men will begin to picture you as a slave overseer. You'll tell them you're just doing your duty. They won't see it that way. The men will become more and more disenchanted with you and you'll become more and more disenchanted with them. Finally you'll give up hope and go to those who understand—the officers."

Gaedtke later told me that what I'd said had made a strong impression on him.

I gave Gaedtke and Wheaton Bertrand Russell's *Appeal to American Conscience,* Felix Greene's *Vietnam! Vietnam!* and Dalton Trumbo's *Johnny Got His Gun.*

The year 1966 became 1967 and the war went on. General Westmoreland asked for more troops, Robert McNamara became euphoric in his optimism and Lyndon Johnson pleaded for "a sign."

By February 1967, Gaedtke and Wheaton were not only anti-brass but anti-Vietnam war.

We talked to everyone who would listen. Soon the entire battalion knew our views. Only a handful showed hostility. Often in the barracks, after lights-out, we would kid about the war. Dick Wheaton, a marvelous mimic, could sound exactly like Lyndon Johnson. He would pretend he was LBJ holding a press conference and the guys would ask questions.

"Mr. President, why are we in Vietnam?"

"Son, to save it from the Communists. Ah want yuh to know that if we have to destroy that country to save it, we will."

"Mr. President, how can we achieve peace in Vietnam?"

"By me and Mr. Minh reasonin' together, son, that's how."

"Mr. President, are you going to send additional troops to Vietnam?"

"Our commitment is firm, son, firm. Ah'm not gonna hide mah tail between mah legs and run. Ah'm willin' to fight to the last drop of yore blood to achieve peace."

"Mr. President, what do you think of the GIs at Fort Sill?"

"Those Communist GIs are a thohn in mah side."

There was little sympathy for student demonstrations and draft-card burnings, but the fact that such things were going on made the guys uneasy. They knew this had not happened during World War II, that there was something different about this war. They learned it from returning veterans who came to Fort Sill to teach jungle warfare. These veterans told of having to kill boys of fifteen—thin, undernourished boys—of having to kill women and children. They described how the victims of napalm and antipersonnel bombs looked. They spoke with awe of the NLF's dedication, shook their heads in dismay over the Saigon regime's unwillingness to defend itself. All of them had experienced firsthand the gulf between the GIs in the swamps and the officers in their air-conditioned clubs.

Every GI dislikes the brass. They dislike the lifers, too, but in a different way. Lifers are the straw bosses of the Army. Most lifers are sergeants, though I have known several forty-year-old PFCs. No sergeant is required to do physical work. The hardest job they have is getting up early and waking the privates; those scheduled for KP are awakened at three-thirty, the others at five. After this the sergeants occasionally have an hour or so of paper work to do, but this is usually handled by clerks. Supervising work details falls on lower ranking sergeants (there are five ranks with an ascending pay scale). Anyone who has ever pulled KP knows that the mess hall is packed from 7 A.M. to noon with sergeants drinking coffee and shooting the breeze.

Once a man gets his foot on the bottom rung of the NCO ladder he's set for life. No job in the world is more secure. Unless the sergeant murders someone in broad daylight with plenty of witnesses around, there isn't much he can do to get himself demoted. The deadly monotony and the aimlessness of their lives drive most of them to drink.

The sergeants are inveterate poker players. And they are poor poker players. They manage to avoid bankruptcy by playing with raw recruits who have never seen a deck of cards before. The recruits are forced into the game and then bullied out of their money.

The sergeant is painfully aware of the gulf between himself and the commissioned officer. Privates don't have to salute him or call him "sir." Nor are sergeants allowed in the officers' club or invited to social functions. The meanest of them take out their frustrations on the enlisted man. Many who weren't cruel to begin with become that way because of the miserable life they lead.

A great many lifers never marry—partly because their pay isn't that good but mainly, I think, because they have become wedded to the barracks. They are comfortable only in the presence of men. Love is a dirty word. Women are alien to them.

The officers, on the other hand, are not only disliked but are held in awe by many of the enlisted men. Most officers come from upper-middle-class backgrounds and tend to look on GIs as savages. Only an officer can be a gentleman.

Officers can be produced in three ways. First, by direct commission. If they are skilled professionals—doctors, engineers or physicists—they are automatically officers. Second, by being graduates of service academies or among those who have taken ROTC. Twenty-five thousand officers —50 percent of the total—make it this way every year. Finally, there's Officer Candidate School. If a man has the educational requirements, he can apply for OCS after basic training.

One of the important exams most OCSers have to pass before being commissioned is the Big Tea Party. The party is usually given by the Colonel's wife, and the would-be officers learn that it's as important to know how to handle a cup of tea as it is to handle a rifle. It is also vital to know whom to be polite to and whom to be rude to. This test is administered at the Pig Party, an event held for each graduating class of the Officer Candidate School at Fort Sill.

The soon-to-be-commissioned officers are told to find the ugliest girls in Oklahoma and invite them to the party. They don't, of course, tell the girls *why* they're invited. Flat-chested girls, enormously obese girls, girls with big noses and harelips and bowlegs—all those to whom nature has been unkind, these are the ones who come to the Pig Party.

They are all girls from surrounding towns, the kind of girls who might never have been out on a date. They have learned to stifle their dreams of romance and have only a shred of secret hope remaining. They must be overwhelmed when glamorous young military men ask to be their escorts to a party. They probably boast about it to their friends, spend days choosing dresses and jewelry.

A friend of mine witnessed one of these parties. He had been pressed into service as a waiter.

The party was only a half hour old. The men were stiff and proper, the girls were shy and awkward but trying to appear gay and sophisticated. Suddenly there was a fanfare of trumpets and an overweight Colonel stepped in front of a microphone. "Will Miss Emmy Lou Simpson please come forward," he said. "She has been chosen Prize Pig of the evening."

Emmy Lou flushed with excitement when she heard her name. She looked expectantly at her escort, misread the expression on his face. She started toward the Colonel, who was holding a plaque. Then she saw the pig's head. And then she realized. She uttered a hoarse little cry, tried to cover her face, but the tears splashed onto her dress as she stumbled out of the room.

It was five minutes before all the girls realized that they had been hoaxed, that they had been invited as pigs. When they had left, the men, as is usual on this time-honored occasion, settled down for a stag party.

Perhaps there are some officers who feel remorse. But since the custom continues year after year, and since there has been no audible outcry against it, it must be presumed that they have choked down their emotions and accepted the Pig Party as part of the process of becoming an officer and a gentleman.

GIs are not famous for their chivalry. Many boast of their conquests and adhere to the 4-F's philosophy. Yet I have never heard an enlisted man who had anything but contempt for what the officers do at the Pig Party.

One of the refreshing things about Army life is the solidarity of GIs against the brass. It shows up in a hundred different ways. The men cover up for each other, lie for each other, are always on the lookout for ways to trick and mislead the brass.

It was common when a GI had been away all night and hadn't returned in time to sign in, for a buddy to sign for him. When the roll was called in the dark during reveille, someone would always yell "Here!" if a friend was missing.

Enlisted medics often gave sick slips (restricting the soldier to light work) in direct defiance of officers who wanted to put feverish men on heavy tasks like humping ammo. If an officer takes a dislike to a GI, few illnesses can keep that GI off hard labor.

In late January 1967 a group of officers raided our barracks. They ordered us to open our wall lockers and announced they were searching for contraband, particularly marijuana. One soldier's locker was so full of pills it looked like a pharmacy; he himself was high at the time and didn't realize what was going on. Everyone wanted to help him. We knew the Army's way of treating addicts is to throw them in the stockade. But it seemed impossible for us to do anything; any movement away from our lockers would have been noticed immediately. Finally a sergeant, a good guy in spite of his stripes, managed to divert the attention of the officers long enough for several of us to stuff our shirts with pills. When they inspected the soldier's locker it was clean.

The use of drugs was widespread at Fort Sill. In the barracks where I was quartered more than 50 percent of the men smoked pot. Speed and Darvon were taken. Some of the clerks got high on correction fluid (used for mimeo stencils). Men on KP often ate large quantities of nutmeg, which causes an enormous jag.

Drugs can erase any awe the enlisted man feels toward the brass. A friend of mine, who was high on something, probably speed, walked into the Colonel's office, sat down, put his feet on the desk, lit a cigarette and blew smoke in the man's face. "Anything I can do for you, John?" he asked.

Even the Colonel's own wife probably didn't dare call him John. He puffed up like a beach ball, his face turned red. He started to call for the MPs and changed his mind. He could handle the situation himself. He walked around his big desk and was bowled over backward by a right to the mouth. By the time the MPs arrived, the Colonel's office was a shambles.

My friend was sentenced to three years in the stockade.

CHAPTER IV   On February 4, 1967, Military Intelligence agents entered our barracks and questioned a number of men about me and my activities in the unit. I felt good, because that meant the brass were getting nervous. Both Paul Gaedtke and Dick Wheaton were helping to promote sentiment against the Vietnam war and we had begun to make plans for a protest on the steps of the officers' club. We chose the officers' club because it was the hangout of those whose ilk in Vietnam were responsible for much of the killing and because it was similar to officers' clubs over there where the brass drank while GIs died.

But we wanted more than three guys for the protest. Three weren't enough. The brass could laugh off three. They couldn't laugh off three hundred. Most of the GIs we tried to get commitments from wavered. They were sympathetic on the one hand, but they were also afraid. We kept trying.

About this time Gaedtke and Wheaton became worried about their DD 98 forms. These Defense Department forms listed organizations the Attorney General considered subversive and asked GIs whether they belonged to any of them or subscribed to their publications. In addition, space was provided for any remarks the GI wanted to make about these organizations. When Gaedtke and Wheaton had first filled out the DD 98 forms they hadn't had any remarks to make, but now it was different—for two reasons: a GI could be fined $10,000 and receive five years in prison for filling the forms out incorrectly; and Military Intelligence agents were well aware of what we were planning to do. Gaedtke and Wheaton didn't want to risk a court-martial because of those DD 98 forms.

On February 9, 1967, they requested that the forms be returned so they could make changes. Under the "remarks" section both wrote that they were opposed to the intervention in Vietnam.

The battery commander was more than upset when he received the revised forms. He thought it would be a blot on his record. He decided to use persuasion. He wrote a letter asking why Paul Gaedtke from Indiana and Dick Wheaton from Michigan were siding with the enemy. He concluded the letter by asking: "Is it really this big, gentlemen? Is it really this big?"

They thought so. And they insisted that the forms be accepted so they would be protected in case of prosecution.

During February our unit was involved in ORT, Operations Readiness Test. We were spending long days in the field in bitter cold. The lieutenant in charge of fire direction control, where Gaedtke and Wheaton were assigned, was a neo-Nazi. Believe it or not, he had a picture of Hitler hanging in his office and a display of Nazi daggers, pistols, helmets and swastikas. He had brought them back from a tour of Germany and boasted about how he would enjoy being the commandant of a concentration camp.

Gaedtke, Wheaton and I felt something ought to be done. We wrote a letter to a newspaper saying there was an officer in our unit who had genuine fascist leanings. We signed our names to the letter.

The letter provoked an investigation. Not of the lieutenant, but of us. We were summoned from the barracks and driven to Military Intelligence. We weren't questioned as a group, but separately. When my turn came I was ushered into a soundproof room and confronted by three burly intelligence agents. One wore a ten-gallon hat and cowboy boots. He did the talking. He told me that a United States Senator had asked for an investigation of Nazi influence at Fort Sill. Then he pulled out a newspaper copy of the letter we had sent. "Did you write this?" he asked.

I had learned by this time not to answer questions. I was certain the story about the senator was phony. The brass weren't interested in prosecuting Nazis, only war resisters. I remained silent.

"You must be interested in cooperating or you wouldn't have written the letter," the fellow in the ten-gallon hat continued. "The senator has asked for an investigation. What should I tell him?"

"Tell him to shove it up his ass." I surely wasn't going to tell officers about the activities of a fellow officer.

Gaedtke and Wheaton were also uncooperative. When ten-gallon-hat offered a handshake, Gaedtke left it hanging in the air. When Wheaton was asked to make a statement, he agreed. A pen and paper were brought and Wheaton wrote, "The statement I wish to make is that I don't wish to make any statements."

By March 1967, Gaedtke, Wheaton and I had decided to rent an apartment in the town near the base—Lawton. A lot of GIs did this; it provided a good deal more freedom than barracks living. Also, Military Intelligence had begun inviting themselves to our late-night discussions and we preferred a little more privacy.

Lawton is a typical Oklahoma town. It has sixty thousand citizens, and in the summer the temperature goes to 105 degrees and stays there. The town has three hundred churches. It also has more bars and pawn shops per capita than any other town I have ever been in. The merchants, who get rich overcharging GIs, are unfriendly toward them, especially if they're black. Blacks can't get served anywhere outside the main strip.

Lawton's sole swimming pool is white-only. When twenty-three black GIs and civilians tried to use it, they were arrested, and General Critz, the Post Commandant, refused the NAACP request to put it off limits for all Fort Sill soldiers.

Most bars in Lawton feature weak beer and juke boxes that blare recordings distributed by a southern outfit called Rebel Records. Rebel Records uses a confederate flag as its label and the racism its songs encourage is typified by titles like "Cajun KKK" and "Lookin' for a Handout."

During the summer of 1967 news of a record burning in Lawton got our hopes up that enlightened citizens had destroyed some of the Rebel Records. But no; it was the week after the Beatles had announced they were more popular than Jesus Christ, and a group of ministers had persuaded their followers to burn Beatle records in the public square. Incidentally, the fire got out of control and almost burned down a city-owned building.

Lawton is a discouraging place. Hot and dusty, populated for the most part with people leeching off GIs, Lawton wouldn't exist if there were no Fort Sill.

The apartment the three of us rented in March was really a shack, but it was better than the chicken coops some of Lawton's GI residents were forced to call home. After we learned that our landlord was one of the major property owners in Lawton and as responsible as anyone in the town for the wretched living conditions, we moved to another place, a five-room apartment over the Sheridan Bar. We fixed the place up the way we wanted it and had plenty of antiwar literature around. It was a good place to come home to after duty.

In April 1967 I was assigned to the Army's ration breakdown section. From 7 A.M. to 5 P.M. we delivered rations to the mess halls in two-and-a-half-ton trucks. What we were actually doing, however, was helping the mess sergeants and the mess officer line their pockets. We were told to falsify records for them. If a particular mess hall fed one hundred men, we were to claim it fed one hundred and fifty. The leftover food was sold to restaurants in Lawton. Reporting this thievery would have done no good, as we were often reminded. Again, it would have been a case of telling officers about a fellow officer and, as we knew, the gentlemen stuck together.

Gaedtke, Wheaton and I each worked from seven to five, then went to bars to talk to other GIs. Often we didn't return to the apartment until two or three in the morning. In the bars, far away from the brass, we had a captive audience. The brass wouldn't have been found dead in the dives we hung around in.

A surprising number of soldiers listened to us, especially when we talked about Vietnam. To some civilians it's just an unpleasant place ten thousand miles away. To GIs it's as close as next week and as real as death. By the end of April 1967 we had recruited four more GIs: Dick Ilg, the battalion intelligence clerk; Stan Ingerman, the battalion medic; Tom O'Reilly, a radio man; and Jim Wood, artillery.

The Case of Captain Howard Levy was receiving national publicity at this time. Levy, an Army doctor, had refused to train men in the Green Berets to go to Vietnam and was court-martialed. All of us felt strongly about Levy's stand; we knew he was probably sacrificing a civilian medical career because of it. Seven of us sent him a telegram: WE

SUPPORT YOU IN YOUR COURAGEOUS STAND AGAINST AMER-
ICA'S DIRTY WAR IN VIETNAM. YOU HAVE RECOGNIZED THAT
AS A DOCTOR YOUR DUTY LIES IN HEALING THE SICK, NOT IN
TRAINING GESTAPO-LIKE GREEN BERET KILLERS. WE WISH
YOU LUCK IN YOUR TRIAL AND HOPE OTHERS WILL FOLLOW
YOUR EXAMPLE.

Soon after sending the telegram Gaedtke, Wheaton and I
were forced to move out of our apartment and back to the
base. Our landlady had seen the antiwar posters in our
apartment. "You may not believe in guns," she said, "but if
you don't clear out you'll see one."

What the landlady didn't understand was that being
against the war in Vietnam did not make a man a pacifist—
in fact it would have been difficult to find three GIs who
believed less in pacifism than we did. But we didn't feel like
arguing the point.

As soon as we moved back on the base antiwar literature
began to appear on the walls of our barracks. The brass ordered MPs to tear it down, but each time they did, more
replaced it.

I was called in front of Colonel Price, the battalion commander, and was asked who was putting the literature on
the walls. Naturally I refused to answer.

The brass decided that more effective action was needed.
I was called away from my job on rations breakdown by
Sergeant Daniel Carnes. Carnes told me the Colonel wanted
the literature I kept in my foot locker.

To my surprise I learned that Carnes already had a key to
my locker and that the locker had been moved into the orderly room. I wasn't going to let them get away with that. I
asked Carnes for some time to think it over, then went to a
friend, who gave me the lock from his locker. Late that
night I entered the orderly room and put the new lock on.

The next morning I was ordered to appear before Lieutenant John Urquhart. He demanded that I open my locker. I told him I would turn over its contents when the books that had been taken from me eight months before were returned. He said he would consider it.

On May 13, my first anniversary in the Army, I was again called to Lieutenant Urquhart's office and ordered to open my locker. I stated that under Army Regulation 381-135 I had a perfect right to keep and read any literature I chose and that therefore his order was illegal. Urquhart pointed to the lieutenant's bar on his shoulder and said, "This makes it legal, Private."

"Like hell it does."

"I'm going to ask you one more time. If you refuse you'll be court-martialed."

"I refuse."

Urquhart called for Sergeant Carnes, and the three of us went to the orderly room. Carnes was carrying an ax. Urquhart posted a guard at the door. It was Jim Wood, the antiwar GI who had joined us a month earlier. He winked at me and I smiled back. Had I been interested in escape, Urquhart would have learned that he had posted the wrong man as guard.

Urquhart ordered Sergeant Carnes to break my locker open, and men all over the barracks heard the rending and splitting of wood as the top of the locker caved in under the ax.

It took Urquhart two hours to go through my literature. There were socialist and revolutionary books, but he also confiscated the *Harvard Crimson,* the *New Republic, Fact* magazine and my American Civil Liberties Union membership card. They were all the same to him.

In the end all that remained was correspondence from my family. Urquhart dropped the letters on the floor and said, "Private, police those up."

CHAPTER V   It was time to get some help from outside. If I was going to be court-martialed, I certainly didn't want to be represented by an Army officer. I had heard that the National Emergency Civil Liberties Committee (NECLC) had a reputation for defending people in trouble with the Government.

NECLC's headquarters are in New York. I phoned and asked if they would send a lawyer and they said they would. They told me I was the first GI who had requested their assistance and that they welcomed the case. Victor Rabinowitz, general counsel for the NECLC, sent a telegram to Colonel Price telling him I would be represented by a civilian lawyer in case of court-martial. Price must have panicked, because he ordered the court-martial for eight o'clock that night.

Just before the court-martial was to begin I was called into Captain Bartholomew's office. Bartholomew was the battery commander, a young man and one of the few officers the enlisted men trusted. He had been assigned to judge the court-martial. He would be the *only* person to judge it. He asked if I had anything to say.

"This trial will be held illegally," I said. "I have civilian counsel."

"Counsel? I wasn't told about that."

"Ask Colonel Price. He's got a telegram from my lawyer."

Bartholomew was angry but he managed to say, softly, "I'll postpone your case ten days."

Most of my friends thought it was a break to get Captain Bartholomew as prosecutor, judge and jury. He had a reputation for fairness. He was known to have given enlisted men a lift into town in his car, a highly unusual thing for any officer to do.

I was skeptical. I believed that the job made the man. No matter how Bartholomew felt, if it was his job to find me guilty, that's what he would do. My main hope rested with the NECLC.

The NECLC was founded in 1951, during the heyday of the McCarthy witch-hunts, when the American Civil Liberties Union was in retreat and refused to handle certain cases. NECLC's first client was the famed illustrator Rockwell Kent, who, in applying for a passport to Ireland, had refused to list his political associations. NECLC won the case and since has been active in thousands of others. It is now helping to handle the case of Martin Sostre, a black liberation fighter who was framed after the Buffalo rebellion in the summer of 1967 and sentenced to forty-one years in prison.

The policy-making body of the NECLC is the National Council, and I'm proud to say I was elected to serve on it in 1969.

But at Fort Sill, Oklahoma, in June 1967 I was just an unknown soldier about to face a summary court-martial. Most summary courts-martial are for soldiers who have gone AWOL. The Fort Sill stockade was packed with AWOL prisoners, many serving a second, third or fourth stretch. The most severe punishment a summary court-martial can give is thirty days at hard labor in the stockade or sixty days at hard labor outside the stockade. There are two other kinds of courts-martial: special and general. A special court-martial can sentence a soldier to as long as six months in prison. And, of course, the general court-martial is the most serious. It is usually given for refusal to obey a direct order and can result in a death sentence.

I had disobeyed an order, but it was an illegal order that violated my rights under the First Amendment to the Constitution. It had also violated Army Regulation 381-135 of the Uniform Code of Military Justice, which states that all GIs have the right to receive any written material they desire and may keep any books, newspapers or pamphlets they choose.

The NECLC sent out a press release announcing that I was to be court-martialed. The release went to most of the antiwar groups in New York City. The only one to respond was Youth Against War and Fascism (YAWF). That anyone would respond amazed me. A representative of YAWF phoned me and asked if I needed help. I said that I did. They agreed to send a delegation to the court-martial. Suddenly I felt very good. Here was I, a private in Fort Sill, Oklahoma, and there were people in New York City who cared enough to come eighteen hundred miles to help someone they had never met before.

Later I learned a good deal about Youth Against War and Fascism. The organization was born in the spring of 1962 when American Nazi party leader Lincoln Rockwell was scheduled to give an address at Hunter College. Some twenty-five students from CCNY, The City College of New York, most of whose parents had been associated with the Old Left, decided to picket Rockwell. These students had been taught how easily fascism can grow from a threat to a reality, and they formed a committee and mimeographed leaflets and distributed them to high schools and universities in the area. To their enormous surprise and satisfaction, more than two thousand people turned out for the demonstration. Most were students, but a few were older people, people in their fifties and sixties and seventies. They remembered the concentration camps. Some had suffered in them and they wore the same prisoners' uniforms they had worn thirty years before. They told the students how happy they were to know there was a group of young Americans with the initiative to put up a fight against the beginnings of a fascist movement.

Lincoln Rockwell never showed up at Hunter College. He had gotten wind of the size of the demonstration.

YAWF grew rapidly that summer and became interested in the war that was developing in Vietnam. Although the United States had only twelve thousand men in Vietnam at the time and they were still being called "advisers," it was clear from reading the back pages of newspapers that a full-scale war was brewing.

YAWF wanted to alert the people of New York—if possible, the people everywhere—about the increasing U.S. military build-up in Asia. Their original name was the Anti-Fascist Youth Committee, but they decided they were as much against imperialist wars as fascism, and changed their name. Within two months of its birth in 1962, YAWF staged the first known public protest anywhere in the United States against the war in Vietnam when it picketed the Information Office of the Army and Marine Corps at Fifth Avenue and Fifty-second Street in Manhattan. YAWF members carried signs reading "Stop the War in Vietnam" and "Bring U.S. Troops Home Now," and passersby stopped and looked at them and said "Where the hell is Vietnam?"

Since 1962, YAWF has been in the forefront of the

struggle against the war in Vietnam. Several of their members have refused induction and are serving jail sentences.

But in June 1967 I knew little about their activities. I was simply grateful they were coming.

My friends in the barracks were elated at the prospect of aid from an unexpected source. There was much speculation as to whether they would be hippie types and arrive carrying guitars and pot. And, of course, we all hoped they would bring some pretty girls.

Three days before the court-martial was to begin, nine members of Youth Against War and Fascism arrived. Instead of guitars and pot, they carried a mimeograph machine. They were young, energetic, bubbling with ideas about how to publicize the trial. Among them was Eddie Oquendo, leader of Blacks Against Negative Dying (BAND). Eddie is now serving a five-year sentence for draft refusal. Others included Key Martin, chairman of YAWF, and his wife Sharon, and Maryann Weissman, YAWF's national coordinator. They set up headquarters in the Lawtonian Hotel.

Gaedtke, Wheaton, Ilg, Ingerman, O'Reilly, Wood and I met with the YAWF members each night and planned strategy. It was decided that if I was found guilty they would hold a demonstration in the courtroom. Of course they didn't know what would happen if they demonstrated. To our knowledge it had never happened at a court-martial.

YAWF called the major wire services, *The New York Times* and the three nationwide television networks. The wire services agreed to come. CBS sent a crew. At least we were going to be heard.

The lawyer NECLC assigned to my case was David Rein. He flew in from Washington the day before the trial. Rein was a World War II Marine Corps veteran, a defender of civil liberties who looked with a jaundiced eye on the Government's increasing infringements of the rights of individuals. Most important for me, he knew military law inside out.

On the morning of the trial the brass called an emergency formation of my unit. The men were warned to stay away from the court-martial. They were told they would be arrested and that charges would be brought against them if they didn't. Five came anyway. They were: Gaedtke, Wheaton, Ilg, Wood and Swallow (our newest recruit). O'Reilly and Ingerman wanted to come but couldn't get off duty.

The trial was held in a stuffy recreation room in Delta Battery of the Second of the Second. The brass tried to make the place look impressive by moving out the pool tables and hanging up an American flag and a large picture of Lyndon Johnson.

Five rifle-toting MPs led me in. I nodded to the five enlisted men and the nine members of YAWF who were seated in the back of the room. The corridor outside the courtroom was crowded with newsmen, TV crews and Army Intelligence agents.

Captain Bartholomew sat behind a desk at the front of the room. Later we learned that Army Intelligence had hidden a tape recorder in his desk. The brass didn't trust anyone the GIs liked.

The first witness called was Lieutenant John Urquhart.

Bartholomew asked: "Lieutenant Urquhart, were you wearing the uniform of an officer when you gave Private Stapp the order to turn over his books?"

"I was."

Urquhart was dismissed. That was the Army's case!

We were surprised, of course. We figured out later that the gangs of newsmen and the presence of YAWF and the five GIs who came in spite of warnings had made the brass nervous. They wanted to rush the trial through as quickly as possible and give us nothing to publicize. In addition, they had already punished me for having a broken foot locker (I hadn't broken it, Carnes had) by fining me and putting me on restrictions for fourteen days.

David Rein had not flown all the way from Washington to let the matter drop so lightly. He called Urquhart back to the stand.

"Lieutenant Urquhart, do you think you violated Private Stapp's First Amendment rights?"

"No."

"Lieutenant Urquhart, what is the First Amendment?"

"I don't know."

"Well, Lieutenant Urquhart, take a guess. You say you didn't violate it, yet you don't know what it is. Take a guess."

"Freedom from illegal search and seizure?"

"No. That's the Fourth Amendment. Now, it's true you violated that also, but we'll cover that in a minute. The First Amendment is freedom of press. Freedom of press, Lieutenant Urquhart. Now—do you know what Army Regulation 381-135 is?"

"No."

"I'll read it to you. 'The Unit Commander shall further insure that there is no interference with U.S. Mails and that any individual in his unit has a right to read and retain commercial publications for his own personal use.' Lieutenant Urquhart, do you know the number of the regulation that permits GIs to give opinions on political subjects?"

"No."

"Lieutenant Urquhart, did you take an oath, an officer's oath, when you entered the Army?"

"Yes."

"Lieutenant Urquhart, did you swear to uphold the Constitution when you took that oath?"

"Yes."

"Lieutenant Urquhart, do you think that the First and Fourth Amendments are part of the Constitution?"

There was no answer.

"Lieutenant Urquhart, did you give the order to break open Private Stapp's foot locker?"

"Yes."

"Lieutenant Urquhart, did Colonel Price know anything about this attempt to take Private Stapp's books?"

This was an important question. If Rein could establish that the order came from Colonel Price, the court-martial would be illegal. The judge of a court-martial has to be at least the same rank as the convening authority, and in this case the judge, Bartholomew, was a captain, and Price was a Colonel. If Rein could prove I had disobeyed Price's orders, not Urquhart's, then the judge was sitting illegally. In addition, the court-martial papers would have been signed illegally, since Urquhart signed them, not Price.

Urquhart said: "It was my order."

Rein dismissed him and called Battery First Sergeant Daniel Carnes. Carnes was the man who had axed open my foot locker. He was a lifer and looked it. He was short, thin, thirty-eight years old, and he could have been mistaken for fifty-eight. As was the custom at courts-martial, he had not been permitted to hear Urquhart's testimony, nor was Urquhart present when Carnes took the stand.

"Sergeant Carnes, did Colonel Price know anything about this order to get Private Stapp's books?"

"Did he know anything about it? Well, it was his idea. We had a conference, Lieutenant Urquhart, myself and Colonel Price. Colonel Price said, 'You've got to get those books out of Private Stapp's foot locker.' "

Carnes was dismissed and Urquhart was recalled.

"Lieutenant Urquhart, did Colonel Price know anything about this attempt to get Private Stapp's books?"

"I've told you he knew nothing about it."

"Lieutenant Urquhart, your own first sergeant has just testified to the opposite. Who's lying, you or he?"

"You're getting me all twisted around."

"Lieutenant Urquhart, I'm not trying to confuse you. I'm trying to clear this matter up. Who gave the order, you or Colonel Price?"

"Well, Colonel Price. He gave the order. But if he hadn't done it, I would have."

Rein asked that the case be dismissed on the grounds that the court-martial papers were improperly signed, that the judge was sitting in violation of the Uniform Code of Military Justice, that one of the Government witnesses had admitted perjuring himself, that Army Regulation 381-135 had been violated and that the Constitution of the United States had been violated.

Captain Bartholomew dismissed all of Rein's motions and ordered the court-martial to continue. I was called to the stand.

I said: "I refused to let them take my literature because the First Amendment of the Constitution of the United States guarantees the right of all Americans to free speech. We GIs say this is not our war. It is Wall Street's war. I'll cite an example: Dow Chemical stocks have soared as a result of the twenty-five million pounds of napalm it sells each month to the military forces in Vietnam. At the same time the death toll of American GIs has risen in proportion to profits and has now reached a new high last week alone of three hundred and thirty-seven. One is haunted by the fact that such companies as Dow profit by the use of napalm, whose only target is man, and that has killed our fellow GIs, sixteen GIs of the First Infantry Division last fall, plus innumerable Vietnamese. Such thoughts prey on our minds and we begin to question and seek answers. Many men in the unit are opposed to the war and have literature similar to what was in my foot locker. I was singled out at random for punishment as an example to others for the purpose of intimidation. The ruling class needs robots in its Army, but we refuse to be unthinking cannon fodder."

The delegation from Youth Against War and Fascism broke into enthusiastic applause and the GIs joined them.

Captain Bartholomew looked embarrassed and called a recess.

Ten minutes later the trial was reconvened. I was found guilty of disobeying an order and sentenced to forty-five days of unconfined hard labor and forfeiture of twenty days' pay. I was also reduced to Private E-1, the lowest rank in the Army.

YAWF broke into angry chanting: "The brass is the tool of Wall Street's rule" and "End the war in Vietnam" and "Bring the troops home now."

Maryann Weissman, her blue eyes flashing, stood in the back of the courtroom and delivered an impassioned speech supporting the right of GIs to organize against the Vietnam war. She said the court-martial's ruling was "a verdict of fear—fear that the nature of the war in Vietnam was being understood by the GIs."

Captain Bartholomew forgot he was addressing a civilian and shouted "At ease!"

When Maryann continued to speak, Bartholomew ordered a black sergeant to remove her from the courtroom. The sergeant looked at his captain and didn't make a move.

The GIs who had witnessed the court-martial were furious. They started chanting with the YAWF members. Outside in the corridor CBS had its cameras trained on the locked door and its tape machines were recording the commotion for the Walter Cronkite show that evening.

Rein was trying to make himself heard over the bedlam. He was saying that the NECLC was appealing the verdict.

Just then Lieutenant Urquhart appeared. Dick Ilg began screaming at him: "Urquhart, you're a liar. We all heard you lie. You tore up the Constitution and trampled all over it."

The courtroom doors opened and Military Intelligence agents poured in. Ilg was arrested and told he would be court-martialed for insulting an officer. He was taken to the barracks and confined there until he could be brought to trial. Meanwhile the Military Intelligence agents were having trouble clearing the YAWF members out of the courtroom. YAWF was proving itself anything but nonviolent. After ten minutes of pushing and shoving and elbowing, YAWF decided their point had been made and walked out.

The morning after the court-martial I reluctantly said goodbye to my allies from Youth Against War and Fascism. The night before, after a pleasant chicken dinner, we had discussed the possibility of their coming back and setting up permanent headquarters to disseminate antiwar literature and to help others who might get court-martialed. Ilg was in custody and we didn't know who might be next. The YAWF contingent agreed to try. Most of them had jobs to get back to, but they said they would think it over in New York and see what could be done.

CHAPTER VI   I was surprised by the news coverage given my court-martial. It reached an international level and gave our movement the kind of publicity it needed to become widely known. *The New York Times* and the New York *Post* carried factual accounts. Papers in Lawton and Oklahoma City bannered the story on page one and were generally hostile. America's underground press gave it prominent and sympathetic attention. The *National Guardian* in New York commissioned Maryann Weissman to write a series of articles and the first was headlined "Anti-War Chants Greet Stapp Verdict." Perhaps most typical of the attitude of wealthy suburbanites, though more embittered because it dealt with a native son, was the editorial of the *Main Line Chronicle* in my home town in Pennsylvania. The editorial was titled "They Call It Freedom of Speech." Here are excerpts:

> Andrew D. Stapp, whose parents live at 559 Heath Rd., was court-martialed at Fort Sill, Oklahoma, last week for refusing to obey an order. He admitted that he let himself be drafted so that he could conduct subversive activities from within. Had this touched-in-the-head young man been a soldier in the Russian or Chinese armies, he would have been summarily executed, war or no war. . . .

Stapp's offense was reduced to mere disobedience. His sentence was not death, but forty-five days at hard labor, forfeiture of $67.50 in pay and reduction to the lowest pay grade. . . .

The present system of government which this person despises grants him the right of freedom of speech, even though his stated aim has been, in his own words, "to organize within the Army against America's imperialistic war of aggression." . . .

The Constitution of the United States allows freedom of the press, but that does not permit this newspaper to vilify. . . .

Still, the Stokely Carmichaels, the flag burners, the vilifiers of Uncle Sam, the riot leaders, the subversives and Stapps invoke the protection of the United States when they take sides with the enemy during times of war.

On the other hand, the European edition of *Stars and Stripes* carried an item from Chicago quoting an American attorney, Hyman M. Greenstein. "Summary courts-martial," said Greenstein, "are the worst abuses against Constitutional rights. You have one officer who is judge, jury and prosecutor and he always finds the man guilty."

When asked to comment on my conviction, Greenstein said: "What a man reads is none of his commanding officer's damn business. Putting on a uniform doesn't mean giving up one's Constitutional rights."

From his home in Wales the venerable philosopher Bertrand Russell issued a statement that made me proud to have taken the stand I did. Mr. Russell said: "I was very interested to learn about the case of Private Andrew Stapp, who has shown great courage in his opposition to the Vietnam war. I earnestly hope that other American soldiers will follow his example."

But in July 1967 I had to think about Dick Ilg, one of our eight members, who was faced with a court-martial.

Dick Ilg, like Gaedtke, was a native of Indiana. He was raised in a conservative Catholic home. His father died when he was in eighth grade, and from then on he helped support his mother. Two years before entering the Army Ilg was involved in a serious accident. He was hit by a speeding car and nearly killed. He was in the hospital for months and the bills for his treatment ran into the thousands of dollars. The insurance company had made an oral agreement to settle out of court for seven thousand dollars.

However, as soon as Dick's name hit the headlines in *The New York Times*—"Second GI Faces Trial at Sill"—the insurance company sent him a letter announcing that it intended to go to trial with his case, not in his home town, but far away from sympathetic friends and relatives to assure an "unbiased" jury. Ilg had no doubt the jury would be told of his antiwar sentiments.

Dick Ilg had counted on that seven thousand dollars, not only to pay hospital bills but because he was planning to get married in a few weeks. He was in love with a girl from Fort Wayne, Indiana, and without the money Dick felt the marriage would have to be postponed indefinitely. So he panicked. In front of reporters he retracted most of the antiwar statements he had made.

On the day of Ilg's trial the brass made sure no civilian or GI sympathizers would be on hand. They posted armed MPs at every entrance to the courtroom, and the proceedings were held in secret. Ilg conducted his own defense, even though the NECLC had volunteered to send Rein from Washington. Dick was afraid to let them. He knew that the House Un-American Activities Committee had branded the NECLC a Communist-front organization.

There was one thing that could have helped Dick Ilg if he had known about it. The Army made certain he didn't know. A well-known CBS news correspondent who had covered my court-martial had sent a telegram to Ilg saying that he had information proving that Urquhart had perjured himself. The correspondent offered to testify in Ilg's behalf.

But the brass didn't deliver the telegram until the trial was over.

A few days before Dick Ilg's trial, Maryann Weissman, who had persuaded her husband Ernie to take his vacation and come with her, returned to Oklahoma. She and Ernie were ready to do whatever they could to help, and began by seeking out antiwar students in and around Oklahoma City, a hundred miles from Fort Sill. A number of students, having read about our opposition to the war, agreed to demonstrate at Ilg's trial. Maryann went to Ilg to tell him about it. She found him at mess, which fact alone caused a sensation at the base, for in no one's memory had a woman, not to mention a young and attractive one, ever entered a mess hall at Fort Sill. Maryann told Dick about the demonstrators and said they would protest outside the courtroom if they couldn't get inside.

Poor Dick refused. He thought that now that he had disavowed his antiwar statements he would be cleared. After all, what had he done but tell the truth about Urquhart? He had called Urquhart a liar and a perjurer, and wasn't that the truth? Urquhart had lied under oath and admitted it.

Ilg was convicted. He was convicted of showing disrespect to an officer. The brass didn't even bother to bring his accuser—Urquhart—into court.

One of the arguments Dick used at the trial was: "I was not speaking to Lieutenant Urquhart, but to John Urquhart, who I felt had just committed a crime." Ilg thought that argument would be the clincher, but it didn't go down with the brass. To them John Urquhart might be a human being, but in his relations with Dick Ilg he was never anything but a lieutenant.

Ilg was sentenced to thirty days at hard labor, fined two-thirds of a month's pay and reduced in rank to E-1.

In the days that followed, the morale of our small group

of dissenters reached its lowest ebb. I felt the Army had definitely won a round. Gaedtke began thinking that bucking the brass was a hopeless undertaking. Wheaton said nothing, but I knew he wasn't happy. Nor were the others. The men in our unit never showed any real hostility, yet they were obviously uneasy in our presence. For one thing, the brass had told them to stay away from us. For another, losers are never very popular. And we had lost twice.

As soon as Ilg could get a night off, he took Gaedtke into Lawton and got drunk on apple wine. When he returned to the barracks he wrote a poem. I can't quote it exactly, but the sense of it was, "I was too cowardly to take the hard road."

Ilg was a good guy, though, and he remained my friend. Some months later he had another opportunity "to take the hard road." He did take it, and his courage was a triumph for all of us.

We didn't have much time to brood over our bad luck because one event followed another so fast that we were kept constantly on the move.

On July 15, 1967, we learned that a Committee for GI Rights (CGIR) had been formed to assist us and any other enlisted men who were in trouble with the brass. Some antiwar people in New York, Buffalo, Milwaukee, Seattle and Cleveland, having read about our courts-martial, and realizing there were many things civilians could do that soldiers couldn't, poured out a lot of energy in a short time and got a committee going. CGIR's most tireless and devoted member was Shirley Jolls, who had been on the staff of the Committee of Inquiry into the Assassination of John F. Kennedy. Shirley contacted lawyers and printers, raised money, solicited support from prominent people. Among the latter were: Brigadier General Hugh B. Hester, U.S. Army (ret.);

H. Rap Brown, Chairman of SNCC; authors Han Suyin and Truman Nelson; editor James Higgins; attorney Florynce R. Kennedy; and U.S. Farmers Association president Fred Stover.

The CGIR printed an imposing brochure titled *Soldiers Against the War* that blew the minds of the brass.

The CGIR asked Paul Gaedtke to make a statement for publication and he jumped at the opportunity. Gaedtke wrote:

> Men like me have no way out of becoming cannon fodder while West Pointers and ROTC men have, to a greater or lesser degree depending on their class background, the power to manipulate their assignments. Any man with the most limited human instincts tries to find a way out of Vietnam. The only way open to me and men of my class is disaffiliation. When I enlisted, I believed we were fighting an enemy, but as I became aware of the genocide and the aggression and the war crimes being committed by the United States, I sought further information. I read everything I could about the war and formed my own opinion: my country is completely wrong in Vietnam.

One day a tall, dark-haired eighteen-year-old came to the barracks looking for me. He bumped into Gaedtke and asked where I was.

"What do you want him for?" Gaedtke asked suspiciously.

"I heard about his stand against the war. I want to help."

His name was Richard Perrin and he had volunteered for the Army. After basic training at Fort Leonard Wood (named for the man who brought out troops against steel strikers in 1919) Perrin had been sent to Fort Sill and was now an E-2 squad leader in charge of a platoon at the armored vehicles repair school.

Perrin was extremely articulate, sensitive, intelligent. He explained why he wanted to oppose the war in an active way. While sitting in a PX cafeteria at Fort Leonard Wood he had heard two sergeants at an adjoining table joking and laughing about their adventures in Vietnam. One told how he had extracted a confession from a captured prisoner—by holding the prisoner's genitals against the superheated engine of a tank.

Richard Perrin had heard so many atrocity stories he couldn't sleep at night. He wrote to his brother—a college student—about his misgivings, and his brother told him about another Fort Sill GI who opposed the war. That was how Perrin learned my name. He became the ninth member of our group.

Dick Ilg and I had begun to wonder when the "hard labor" part of our sentences was going to be enforced. Then, on July 22, 1967, we were ordered to the Judge Advocate General's office and told we were going to see the big man himself, the invisible man behind all courts-martial at Fort Sill, the man who stage-managed the entire show, Colonel George Robinson. Robinson was a full bird colonel, which meant he wore an eagle instead of an oak leaf on his shoulder, and when you met him you always felt that eagle was foremost on his mind and he hoped you would recognize in him the living embodiment of that indomitable symbol.

Colonel George Robinson handled so many courts-martial in 1967 that he achieved national fame. In the winter of 1968, after fourteen-, fifteen- and sixteen-year sentences were doled out to the San Francisco Presidio rebels (whose "crime" was a short sit-down strike in protest over the murder of a fellow prisoner), Robinson was flown to California as an adviser. But so many threats were made on his life that he had to be transferred.

Ilg and I didn't get to meet Robinson. Instead we were

greeted by Colonel Irwin, the 214th Group Commander. Irwin told us the hard-labor part of our sentences had been dropped.

"You guys were becoming martyrs," he said. "I'm tired of all the publicity."

"Don't expect thanks," I said. "We didn't court-martial ourselves."

"Always a wise guy, aren't you, Stapp?"

As we were leaving 214th Group Headquarters a captain met us and took Ilg aside. Although the captain tried to keep his voice down, I heard him say, "Ilg, there was something funny about your court-martial. I don't think you got a fair shake."

"Who was that?" I asked Ilg when the captain had left. "He seemed like a fair-minded guy."

"He was the judge," Ilg replied.

When Ilg and I talked it over afterward we figured the reason the hard labor was dropped was that GIs must have been beefing about the sentences we had received much more than we had thought. The CGIR booklet had been distributed all over the base and it presented a pretty clearcut case for us.

Still, we were glad not to have the sentences hanging over our heads. "Unconfined hard labor" means that after your regular day of hard work is finished at 5 P.M., you have to keep on working until 11 P.M., then be out of bed the next morning at five to start all over again. Forty-five uninterrupted days of this, or even thirty, is not a lot of laughs. We probably would have been assigned to the motor pool, washing trucks and changing heavy tires.

There are a lot of bad jobs given a GI on unconfined hard labor. Humping ammo is one. The ammo boxes weigh more than a hundred pounds and it is not uncommon for a man to lift a thousand of them a day. The boxes, which each contain two 105-mm shells, are picked up at a large ammunition dump and loaded into trucks to be distributed on the firing range. The ammo dump is a dangerous place. GIs are warned not to carry matches, pistols or radios and are searched before being allowed to enter (many of the shells can be detonated by transistor radio waves). If the ammo dump blew up, it would level most of Fort Sill.

GIs humping ammo have to unload *all* the boxes from the truck at each station of the firing range, not just the boxes meant for that station. At each station the boxes are counted by the officer in charge, then those intended for other stops are reloaded onto the truck; at the next station this silly process is repeated.

Except for combat, however, KP is the worst duty a soldier can get. Anyone from sergeant on up is exempt from KP, and that is one very good reason most GIs would like to make sergeant.

The day of a soldier on KP begins at 3:30 A.M. with a sergeant shining a light in his face. The soldier shivers into his uniform, staggers over to the mess hall and waits outside for an hour until the cooks arrive. Enlisted men have often been disciplined for breaking into the mess hall because they chose not to freeze on winter mornings while waiting for the cooks to show up.

There is usually a real mean cook and a real nice cook, but the nice one is never in charge. The cooks work two shifts: 5 A.M. to noon, and noon to 9 P.M. The GI on KP works both shifts.

The implements used in a mess kitchen are like nothing ever seen in a home. The spoons are like shovels and the forks are as long as a man's arm. There's a machine for peeling potatoes and another for mashing them. But there is no machine for washing dishes. They are done by hand. Since a GI washing dishes has his hands in water fifteen hours a day, he doesn't want the water kept too hot. The cooks, however, who are really kitchen foremen, keep the water boiling hot to make certain the grease comes off everything. At the end of a dishwasher's day his fingernails are like rose petals and his hands are torn to pieces because the soap has too much lye in it.

Whenever a GI thinks he has caught up on the dishes and can sneak a smoke, the cooks tell him to mop the floor. The floors are mopped a dozen times a day.

Enlisted men sometimes get so frustrated on KP that they take it out on the food. I have seen two hundred pounds of potatoes dumped into the peeler and left there until they were the size of peas. I saw a soldier put his muddy boot into a vat of orange juice. Another time a group of GIs beat up a room full of bananas until they were nothing but pulp.

These were the jobs we could look forward to in serving our sentences.

CHAPTER VII   A number of things happened during the last two weeks in July: Paul Gaedtke went AWOL and was thrown into the stockade; Richard Perrin was caught in town without a pass and court-martialed; Maryann Weissman was almost lynched by a Lawton mob; and I was court-martialed a second time.

My personal life also took an important turn. Despite the excitement and preoccupation of fighting the brass, I was lonely. I was a GI without a girl, not even someone back home to write to. My changing political views had forced a rupture with the girl I was fond of in college, and the wrench was something I knew I couldn't go through again. Having decided that I could only love a girl whose politics I shared, I was resigned to finishing out my Army tour before looking for romance. It never occurred to me that I might find it in Lawton, Oklahoma.

Of all the scenes of turbulence and struggle against the war that had crowded into the press, one photo had strangely stuck in my mind for nearly a year. It was a picture of a girl being dragged out of a Congressional hearing for yelling "Murderer!" at a Marine Corps general. When my association with YAWF began, it startled me to find out that the girl whose features I had memorized was editor of

YAWF's magazine, *The Partisan*. Her name was Deirdre Griswold.

I followed her articles from London and Stockholm on the International War Crimes Tribunal, at which Johnson, Westmoreland and that Marine Corps general were being tried *in absentia* by a group of internationally prominent intellectuals for aggression, genocide and other crimes against the Vietnamese people. Deirdre had been invited to work on the tribunal by its founder, Bertrand Russell.

A few days before my next court-martial I learned that she was back from Sweden and would be in the delegation from YAWF which was driving down from New York for the trial.

The five GIs who had been at my first court-martial in defiance of the brass were all penalized in one way or another. Gaedtke was taken off his job in fire direction control and assigned to guard duty. As a Spec Five, he wasn't used to being treated this way. Spec Fives are supposed to be on a par with sergeants and are generally respected for their superior knowledge and skills. When Gaedtke refused to accept the demotion, he was restricted to barracks.

Paul Gaedtke was outgoing, active, always on the move. Restricting him to barracks was like locking a claustrophobe into a closet. Within a week he was AWOL.

Gaedtke went into Lawton and stayed there. He took a job in a discotheque. There were a lot of AWOL GIs in Lawton. It wasn't hard for them to get jobs if they were willing to work for low wages, which is what their circumstances forced them to do and which is why most employers were willing to hire them.

Gaedtke had saved some money and the first thing he did was buy a used motorcycle. It made him feel good to zoom off on country roads, pretending he was free. But one day when he was racing down the highway he tangled with a truck. He wasn't hurt much but the accident called attention to his whereabouts and the Army got him.

The stockade is where most AWOL GIs end up sooner or later. The Fort Sill stockade is a muddy field surrounded by barbed wire and has crude barracks at one end. Two fences tipped with barbed wire, with another roll of barbed wire wedged in between, make escape virtually impossible. But in case someone is willing to tear himself to ribbons to try, the stockade has a tower in each corner and the towers are manned twenty-four hours a day by armed guards.

Time spent in the stockade does not count as time spent in the Army. If a GI is in for two years and spends a year in the stockade, it is three years before he is out of the Army. Many civilians, whose knowledge of stockades comes from watching war movies, think all the prisoner does is lounge around all day or play basketball. That isn't true. The prisoners work. And they don't get paid for it, which is one small consolation for the GI on KP.

One of the jobs the prisoner gets is operating the gluppeta-gluppeta machine, which makes concrete for parking lots. Or he might be sent to cut down trees and clear away brush, working under a guard armed with a shotgun. Many of the guards seem to enjoy their work.

Although it is virtually impossible to escape from inside the stockade, escapes from work details on the outside are fairly common and attest to the daring and ingenuity of GIs. I know of a prisoner who was being transferred from one stockade to another by airplane.

"What do I do if the plane starts to crash?" he asked the guard.

"You put on a parachute."

"How do you work the darn thing?"

"I'll show you."

The guard fastened the parachute, gave a quick lesson on how to operate it, then stood dumbfounded as his prisoner leaped to freedom.

Gaedtke later told us that life in the stockade was not really much worse than regular Army life. What threw many of the GIs, especially those from small towns, where respectability is the aim of most families, was the disgrace of being in the stockade. The first thing the brass gave stockade prisoners was a copy of the Bible. Gaedtke saw a lot of soldiers reading their Bibles with tears in their eyes.

In spite of their strict family backgrounds, many prisoners ate up Gaedtke's ideas about Vietnam. What convinced them, I think, was the absolute realization of which class of Army society they belonged to. No matter how serious his crime, an officer is seldom sent to the stockade.

After receiving his Bible the GI is sent to see the stockade psychiatrist, on the supposition that anyone who would go AWOL must be emotionally troubled. The psychiatrist pegged Gaedtke a "passive aggressive," which we found hard to figure out.

Gaedtke spent only three days in the stockade on this occasion, though he would later return for a much longer stay as a result of his antiwar activities. In July 1967, however, choosing expedience over principle, the Army decided Gaedtke's specialized skills were more needed in Blanding, Utah, where work was going on in preparation for firing a large missile, than they were at Fort Sill operating the gluppeta-gluppeta machine.

With a twenty-four-hour guard to make sure he didn't go AWOL again, Gaedtke was flown to Utah. The missile he helped launch, which was supposed to land in White Sands, New Mexico, landed instead in the Mexican desert, touching off a diplomatic crisis.

When Gaedtke returned to Fort Sill in September he was

a free man; free to again organize antiwar dissent, an activity he embraced with missionary zeal.

Richard Perrin, the eighteen-year-old who had not liked what he had heard at Fort Leonard Wood, turned out to be one of our strongest activist allies. About the time Gaedtke was going AWOL, Perrin was calling a press conference. He issued a statement that received nationwide publicity and that upset the brass more than a little. Here's what Dick Perrin said:

> Before I enlisted in the Army, I had been to only one anti-war meeting, seeing the film *The Time of the Locust* and hearing the tape of Bertrand Russell's *Appeal to the American Conscience*. I couldn't believe the atrocities I had seen and heard and pushed them into the back of my mind.
>
> However, at Fort Leonard Wood, I overheard two sergeants joking about Vietnam and the barbarities one of them committed there. He told of torturing a prisoner in order to extract information. Later I heard other accounts of equally inhuman actions.
>
> I was being trained as a truck mechanic and was on my way to Fort Sill to work on armored trucks and self-propelled artillery. I realized I was being trained to support these atrocities. At this point I decided to find out for myself whether there was any justification for this war. Everyone said there was, but they couldn't tell me what it was.
>
> I wrote my brother and he told me he knew of no sane purpose for the war. He said I should look up Private Andy Stapp, who had just been court-martialed for anti-war activities, though the Army didn't call it that. I went to Private Stapp and learned I wasn't alone.
>
> The anti-war movement had answers. I explained them to friends in the barracks and they shook their heads and said "Don't get involved," and they had what-can-we-do expressions on their faces. I told them what they could do. They could refuse to fight in this awful war.
>
> I hope the people of the United States will wake up to the fact that they are being led through a period that will one day

be called the darkest in our history. The world's people will
condemn the United States, just as they condemn Hitler. I
hope we anti-war GIs can count on support in our efforts.

Three days after his statement appeared in newspapers
from coast to coast Perrin went into Lawton with Tom
O'Reilly and Dick Wheaton to visit Ernie and Maryann
Weissman, who had set up headquarters in a motel room
and were beginning to organize student support for the GI
struggle.

On the way back to base Wheaton's car was stopped by
Military Intelligence agents. The three soldiers were told to
show their passes. Wheaton and O'Reilly produced theirs.
Perrin had forgotten to pick his up and was taken into custody.

Being caught without a pass is a trivial offense in the
Army. Many soldiers at Fort Sill never bothered to pick one
up when they went into town. If your first sergeant caught
you, and if he liked you, he wouldn't say a word. If he disliked you, he bawled you out. And if he really hated you, he
put you on KP.

Richard Perrin was court-martialed.

Seven days later he was found guilty and led away, hand-
cuffed, with an M-16 rifle at his back. The guard who had to
hold the rifle was so upset that *he* went AWOL and wasn't
picked up until a month later.

The brass kept Perrin in solitary confinement for fifteen
days. They tried a number of ways to break him. Chaplains,
playing the soft-cop role, told him he should right himself
with God (most chaplains at Fort Sill referred to the NLF
as "gooks" and "Chinks"). When the men of the cloth
failed, captains and majors played hard cop: "You'll rot
forever down here if you don't retract that statement."

Such was hardly the case. Perrin's antiwar friends were
active enough to get people stirred up about what the brass

were doing, and they finally had to let him out. He was shipped to Germany the next day. What he did there will be reported later.

Ernie Weissman's vacation ended the day after Richard Perrin was taken into custody. Ernie had to go back to New York. He didn't want to be separated from Maryann but he had seen enough to urge her to stay on and continue the work they had begun together. He made arrangements for Key Martin, chairman of Youth Against War and Fascism, to come to Lawton and lend a hand. Students from hundreds of miles around had begun to bombard the motel headquarters with letters, phone calls and visits. It was too much for Maryann to handle alone.

A large contingent of students and GIs were on hand in Lawton to greet Key Martin when he arrived. Martin was twenty-four years old and looked a lot younger. Tall and gangling, with a shock of straight brown hair that kept falling into his eyebrows, he wore thick-rimmed glasses that gave his face a solemn expression. Key Martin was a whirlwind, a bubbling, boiling, hyperactive bundle of human energy that never walked when it could run. Key and Maryann were people who got things done, and there were always things that needed doing. Like preparing press releases and advising students and arranging for as many people as possible to attend the July 31 court-martial.

Key Martin moved into the room next to Maryann and I visited them the first day I could get a pass. When I arrived they were reading an article in the *Oklahoma City Times* that was headlined "Woman Using Lawton as Anti-War Drive Base."

The article pinpointed the "woman's" address and assured citizens that she was under "constant surveillance." The article quoted Lawton Police Chief Hennessey as saying:

"I'm pretty frustrated. We don't know what we can do. If I knew anything more I could do I'd sure do it."

About an hour later I glanced out the window and learned that Chief Hennessey didn't have to do anything. Someone else was doing it for him. A radio announcer from a local station was standing in front of Maryann's window and saying, "A crowd is gathering here . . ."

No crowd had gathered until he had started to talk.

The announcer's urgent tone attracted a considerable audience. Bartenders, used-car salesmen, pawnshop owners, street-corner loungers, all the citizens who make up a small southern Army town began to congregate around him. Within fifteen minutes, more than three hundred people were pushing and elbowing for position. The crowd became ugly and the announcer left. Soon there was kicking and hammering at the door.

"Get out of town, you Communist," someone yelled.

"Remember how we used to handle traitors?"

"I remember! Yes, sir, I remember!"

"Do we kill her first? Or do we fuck her and then kill her?"

Abruptly the noise stopped. We heard the motel manager pleading with the crowd to disperse. "My life savings are tied up in this place," he said. "Please don't tear it down."

There were angry mutterings, but the kicking and hammering stopped. I peered out the window and saw that the crowd had retreated a dozen or so yards.

Then a knock at the door sounded. It was the manager. Maryann opened the door a crack, keeping the safety chain attached. The manager said we would have to leave, that *we* were the cause of the disturbance.

Maryann reminded him that the room was paid for in advance and slammed the door in his face. We heard him once again begin to plead with the crowd.

The police arrived—finally. They managed to back the mob away a few more yards but made no attempt to disperse them.

Maryann phoned a lawyer in Denver. The lawyer called the Oklahoma Attorney General and demanded that we be given better police protection. The Attorney General phoned Chief Hennessey, who said that if the people of Lawton wanted to stay on the street and have a little fun, then that was their right.

Afternoon turned to night and night to dawn. It was almost 5 A.M. and I was due back at base. Only the police and a dozen or so drunks remained. I opened the door and stepped outside and two men materialized out of the shadows. "When are they going to get out, Stapp?" one of them asked.

They looked so much like FBI agents that I figured they were. I didn't answer the question.

At 8 A.M. Maryann Weissman and Key Martin were arrested for trespass. They were booked, mugged, fingerprinted and put in separate cells that contained four other prisoners, a sink and a toilet. When Maryann's purse was taken from her and examined by two policemen, she heard one of them say, "Look, Horace, she's got Russian money!"

The policeman was looking at New York City subway tokens.

The Lawton *Constitution* and the *Daily Oklahoman* filled their front pages with stories and pictures. They found Maryann especially photogenic. There was a picture of Maryann being fingerprinted, of Maryann being questioned, of Maryann behind bars. They wrote about how she looked, what she wore, what she had for lunch. I found only one relevant line. The Lawton *Constitution* said: "The arrest is an attempt to silence her work in opposing the Vietnam war."

Key and Maryann were released after fourteen hours in jail. Outside the jail a group of antiwar students from the University of Oklahoma were on hand to greet them. The students burst into cheering when Key and Maryann appeared. They were driven to Norman, an Oklahoma City suburb, where they set up a new headquarters and began making plans for a demonstration at the upcoming courts-martial of Richard Perrin and Andy Stapp.

Several hundred University of Oklahoma students had asked me to come to their campus on July 15 to speak against the war. I had looked forward to it because it was an opportunity to form a bond between students and GIs, a bond I felt was warranted by our positions. We were the ones the Government had earmarked for Vietnam.

The brass heard about my speech and decided to prevent it. On July 14 I returned to the barracks to find ammunition scattered on my bunk. I also found two officers waiting for me.

Having *anything* scattered on your bunk is a violation of the Uniform Code of Military Justice. Bunks are supposed to be as neat as a row of coffins. The Army thinks it's good for morale.

"This time you're really in trouble, Stapp," said one of the officers.

"I didn't do this and you know it."

"You're responsible for your own bunk."

"Fingerprint the ammo. You'll find out I didn't handle it."

"You were probably smart enough to wear gloves."

The officer told me there would be an investigation and that meanwhile I was confined to base. I asked for permission to fulfill my commitment at the University of Oklahoma but they said no.

The next night there was a movie at the post theater, *The*

Gold Rush, one of Charlie Chaplin's early pictures. I went to my sergeant, Daniel Carnes (the same sergeant who had embarrassed Lieutenant Urquhart at my first court-martial), and asked if I could go.

"Why not?" Carnes said. "You're restricted to post, not barracks."

Still smiling over the scene where Chaplin eats his shoe, I was preparing for bed when the officers came. I was told that I would be court-martialed for violating barracks restriction and that the court-martial would be held on July 31.

The next two weeks were hectic. I called NECLC in New York and they agreed to send a lawyer, Rudolph Schware, from Denver to represent me. They also said they would make sure the case received wide publicity. They wanted to tell the American people about the arbitrary and punitive ways the Army uses courts-martial to whip dissident GIs into line. The television networks, the wire services and newspapers from all across the country agreed to cover my trial.

Then I began to receive a flood of letters, and this made the brass (who were opening and reading them) nervous. A few of the letters called me a "subversive" but most were friendly. Some of the writers said they were coming to Fort Sill to join the planned student-GI-veteran demonstration.

And what a demonstration was planned! Key and Maryann had recruited dozens of students. My allies on base, led by Dick Wheaton, had organized almost two hundred GIs. Some fifty Oklahomans—veterans of World War II and Korea and Vietnam—who were familiar with the Army's brand of justice decided to be heard too.

The vision of swarms of demonstrators converging on Fort Sill was too much for the brass to take. On July 29, two days before the court-martial, they moved simultaneously on three fronts: GIs were told they would be arrested if they joined the demonstration; civilians were warned that the Lawton police took a dim view of "outside agitators" who intended to "invade" their town; and Key and Maryann were handed bar orders forbidding them to enter the base.

The morning of the court-martial broke clear and hot. At 6 A.M., with Key and Maryann in the lead car, a caravan of jam-packed automobiles began the hundred-mile journey from Oklahoma City to Fort Sill. It was escorted by carloads of Norman police, state police and Military Intelligence agents.

At 214th Group Headquarters, where the trial was to be held, the opponents faced each other in tense silence. The building was surrounded by MPs with fixed bayonets. A helicopter whirred overhead. Intelligence agents milled among the crowd of sympathetic GIs who had gathered outside the court-martial building.

I sat on the bunk in my barracks staring at two armed guards. The guards evidently thought I might try to escape. Their pistols were drawn.

Television crews flashed bulletins on the progress of the caravan en route from Oklahoma City and recorded the increasingly hostile barbs being tossed back and forth in front of the headquarters building. The brass were becoming more and more uneasy. Perhaps at this point many of them wished they didn't have to face a confrontation, but since they had planted the ammo on my bunk and initiated the court-martial, by God, they were going through with it.

But the brass prefer a trial that can be carried on quietly, without controversy, where the GI defendant is isolated because civilians are unaware of his plight. It is then that the brass go hog-wild and show no mercy whatsoever—for example, the six- and ten-year sentences given William Harvey and George Daniels for "disloyal words." During a discussion with a group of fellow marines these two black men had *talked* about why it was wrong to go to Vietnam.

One of the judges at their court-martial became so outraged by the statement of a witness on the status of black people in the United States that he said: "I must profess that I am profoundly shocked. Profoundly shocked. I was raised with Negroes. I have known Negroes all my life. I have a very high respect for Negroes and I do not believe one-tenth of what I read. We speak of Negro ghettos, and I have been in the Negro section of town many times and I don't believe they have it so bad there."

This same judge rejected the motion of the defense to dismiss the case on the constitutional grounds of violation of freedom of speech and freedom of assembly with a classic statement of fascist jingoism: "A very strict and narrow interpretation of the First Amendment would certainly support the argument you have made. But it recalled to my mind a statement, and I don't recollect right now who made it, but 'My country, right or wrong, is still my country,' and I think that as a matter of constitutional law that pretty well wraps up the expression of what the situation is."

The caravan from Oklahoma City never reached the court-martial. As they turned off the expressway onto the ramp that led to the base they were halted by road blocks manned by MPs and federal marshals. Key and Maryann were told they had violated the bar orders and were placed under arrest. Along with a dozen others they were taken inside the base to the Provost Marshal's office. The students who had come to demonstrate were ordered to go home. For a long time they refused, and the result was a big traffic jam.

At 9 A.M., with two pistol-carrying guards at my back, I was led through the swarm of friends and the cordon of MPs to the 214th Group Headquarters building for the trial. I felt good and the MPs looked angry when the guys began shouting encouragement. Inside the courtroom I shook hands with my attorney, Rudolph Schware, and he said, "Don't worry."

At the same time I was sitting down to await my court-martial, Colonel Melford Wheatley, Provost Marshal, was telling the group that had been brought in with Key and Maryann that under no circumstances would they be allowed to attend the trial. In that group were Eddie Oquendo and Deirdre Griswold. Deirdre had been chosen to do the talking.

"Are we under arrest?" she asked Wheatley.

"No. Only Martin and Mrs. Weissman are. But none of you are going to be attending any courts-martial today. Your intention is to disrupt and demonstrate and we won't have it."

"Are you a mind reader? Who says we intend to disrupt and demonstrate?"

Colonels aren't accustomed to being questioned. People take orders from them and keep quiet about it. Who did this upstart daughter of permissive parents think she was?

"I've made my decision, young woman."

Deirdre persisted: "The Army said this was to be an open trial. It is an open trial, isn't it?"

Just then they were interrupted by the sounds of a scuffle. Eddie Oquendo, who is six feet, four inches tall, was holding a camera and a portable tape recorder above his head and a pair of MPs were jumping around him trying to reach the forbidden equipment. Eddie had been taping the meeting and now he was smiling like a smug cat safe in a tree while terriers went through the futile motions of barking and leaping. Eddie's friends began cheering him and Wheatley's face turned red. He ordered the MPs to stop, then called a larger contingent of MPs and told them to escort the "troublemakers" off the base. Key and Maryann had already been taken into custody by Federal marshals.

At 214th Group Headquarters the Army was beefing up its defenses. The MPs were fortified with cans of Mace, tear-gas guns and fire hoses.

The court-martial got under way at 9:30 A.M. The Army's case was cut and dried. An officer told how he had restricted me to barracks because of the ammo scattered on my bed, and a second officer testified that I had violated this order by attending a movie at the post theater.

The Army rested its case. Now it was Rudolph Schware's turn. He had headed the Trade Union Unity League during the 1930s, had fought in the Spanish Civil War, and had been an Army officer in World War II. Like my first lawyer, David Rein, Schware was an expert on military law. I hoped that, unlike Rein, he could win a not-guilty verdict. I knew his chances were slim. The brass wanted me in the stockade. In addition, I knew that 95 percent of courts-martial are decided against the accused.

The group the Provost Marshal had ordered off the base was escorted to the expressway by an Army helicopter and by MPs who followed them in jeeps. Then the MPs turned back toward the base and so did the protesters.

They almost made it to 214th Group Headquarters. After a wild, full-throttle, pedal-to-the-floor chase along the dusty streets of Fort Sill they were forced off the road less than three hundred yards from their destination. Minutes later they were back in the Provost Marshal's office facing an irate Melford Wheatley. Wheatley said they would be held until the trials were over, and Deirdre demanded the right to call an attorney. She phoned the NECLC lawyer in Denver and was told that the Army had no authority over them and that they could not be held against their will. The lawyer said they weren't even required to give their names.

They had already given their names the first time they had been taken to the Provost Marshal's office, and while they were being escorted off the base Wheatley had had bar orders prepared for each of them. The trouble was, Wheatley didn't know which name fitted which person; he read the names from the bar orders but was greeted by silence.

The comedy continued. The group decided that since they were being held illegally, they would leave. Wheatley ordered a half-dozen MPs to guard the door. Standing stiff, rifles at the ready, the MPs barred the exit. There they remained, at attention, for the entire day.

As time wore on, Wheatley began to think. There had to be a legal way to hold the group. Then he got an idea. He scratched all the names off the bar orders and substituted John Doe or Jane Doe on each of them. He told an MP to serve the revised bar orders, but everyone folded his or her arms and refused to accept them. The MP then touched each person with a bar order, let go of it, and littered the floor with paper. The courts-martial were over when Wheatley finally let them go.

Standing outside the 214th Group Headquarters and trying to figure a way to circumvent the MPs and the fire hoses were some fifty GIs. The brass were particularly fearful of them. They could dismiss other demonstrators as "Communist-inspired," but not the GIs, many of whom had served in Vietnam. Although the GIs had been threatened with arrest if they showed up, it was soon clear that this was a hollow bluff.

I think the GIs came for two reasons: they were angry over what was clearly an attempt to frame a fellow soldier; and they wanted to vent their frustrations over the extra work they had been forced to do for the past month. Everyone in my company had been working from 8 A.M. to 11 P.M. getting billets ready for a group of West Point cadets who were coming to Fort Sill for a three-day visit. We buffed floors until they gleamed like silver, cleaned windows until they seemed transparent, painted whole buildings so the soon-to-be officers would feel comfortable and at home. (Oddly, when the cadets did arrive they complained of finding mounds of dirt and rusty iron bars and frogs and caterpillars and cockroaches sharing their beds.)

Rudolph Schware began his cross-examination by questioning the officer who said that he had confined me to barracks.

"Lieutenant, did you place Private Stapp on post restriction or barracks restriction?"

"On barracks restriction."

The lieutenant was dismissed and Sergeant Daniel Carnes was called.

"Sergeant, was Private Stapp on post restriction or barracks restriction?"

"On post restriction."

"Sergeant, on July 15 did you give Private Stapp permission to attend a movie at the post theater?"

"I did."

The Army had no case at all. And with a large group of newsmen and GIs waiting outside, they decided to admit it. I was found not guilty.

I walked out of the courtroom and onto the grounds, raising a clenched fist in victory.

The guys let out a cheer! It made me feel very good. I knew they weren't just cheering me—many of them didn't even know me—they were cheering the victory of an enlisted man over the brass.

As I walked past them on the way to the jeep that had brought me to my trial some of them shook my hand, a few slapped my back, others asked if I planned to return for Perrin's trial that afternoon. I said that I did.

When I reached the jeep the driver was simonizing it.
"What are you doing that for?" I asked.

The driver grinned and said, "The Colonel wanted it to look good on television when we drove you to the stockade."

CHAPTER VIII   Oklahoma is a great state to be tried in. In 1965 two members of the State Supreme Court were arrested for taking bribes.

Key Martin and Maryann Weissman were brought before Federal Judge Luther Bohanon on August 2, 1967, in Oklahoma City, and were charged with trespass for having ignored the Fort Sill bar order. Bohanon set trial for August 25 and freed them on one-thousand-dollar bail. Freedom in Oklahoma meant they had to meet with a probation officer twice a day, they couldn't leave Oklahoma City, they couldn't associate with anyone from YAWF and they couldn't talk to students or GIs.

Dick Wheaton and I and a few others began meeting with Eddie Oquendo and Deirdre Griswold and the rest of the antiwar civilians who had come to Fort Sill. Out of these meetings grew the concept of organizing enlisted men into a union that would fight for GI rights and against the brass and the war. Because of circumstances and publicity, my name had become a sort of symbol of the growing unrest among GIs, and we decided that I should head the union. In addition, I had received letters and cables from hundreds of soldiers in places as far removed as Fort Story, Virginia, Fort Jackson, South Carolina, Fort Leonard Wood, Missouri, Fort Dix, New Jersey, Fort Hood, Texas, and Fort Campbell, Kentucky, all supporting our stand against the war and saying they would desert rather than go to Vietnam. We sensed a ground swell of dissent, and subsequent events proved us correct. Let me give an example.

According to Defense Department figures, which are always suspect (if the casualty figures issued each week are correct, the United States has killed or wounded every man, woman and child in Vietnam twice), 190,000 GIs either deserted or went AWOL in 1967 and 1968. These soldiers, many of whom are still on the loose, form a sort of twilight cadre, always on the move, without officers or chain of command, a lost army, hunted and rejected, with its own ethos, its underground, its legal-aid procedures, its sources of funds, its spokesmen and its secret meeting places—a fragmented, unrecognized group of men who together amount to more than twelve combat-strength divisions in the United States alone, not to mention the deserter colonies in Canada, Mexico, Sweden, France, England and Japan. But this is a fact the brass like to ignore or play down. They say Vietnam deserters are a minuscule minority, cowards, a group unworthy of the traditions of Barbara Frietchie and Patrick Henry and George Washington.

My first job was to answer the letters and cables and find out what kind of sentiment there was for a union. Deirdre helped me write the letters, and we began to see quite a lot of each other.

The brass knew what I was doing. They read the letters that were sent to me before I did. On August 10, 1967, I was called before Colonel Price. He rubbed his hands together and said: "Stapp, you're not in shape. I'm putting you on permanent ammo-humping duty. The men there don't have much upstairs, but they do have strong backs."

My back got strong, too, because the only job I had from

that time on was humping ammo. I enjoyed it. The GIs who did the ammo humping were good fellows to be around. Equally important, it wasn't hard to convince them that the Army and the war stank.

Most of the ammo humpers were black. No matter how much education a black man had, the Army gave him the worst jobs. Almost all the black ammo humpers had graduated from high school. Two of them had degrees from Howard University. With the exception of myself, none of the white ammo humpers had gone past the tenth grade.

The stand taken by Key Martin and Maryann Weissman had lifted the spirits of a lot of GIs. Now they saw that civilians were willing to go to jail fighting for GI rights. Key and Maryann received messages of support from all around the world. It was because of this development, because of the international scope of resistance that was beginning to coalesce around the struggle at Fort Sill, that we realized this was not just an episode but an entire movement.

U.S. Attorney John Raley subpoenaed me to Key and Maryann's August 25 trial. Key and Maryann were represented by American Civil Liberties Union lawyers.

Every prosecution witness was an Army man. Even General Charles (Charlie) Brown was called to testify. The General, his tone solemn, said that Maryann and Key had jeopardized troop morale at Fort Sill and that there had been "rumblings" on the base. He said he had discussed these rumblings with the Pentagon "before making my agonizing decision to bar Mrs. Weissman and Mr. Martin from Fort Sill."

The American Civil Liberties Union lawyers hammered on one point: Key and Maryann couldn't be guilty of trespass because they hadn't been on the base when they had been arrested; they had been on a ramp leading off the expressway.

But Key and Maryann weren't really being tried for trespass and everyone knew it.

In delivering his decision Judge Bohanon called the trespassing charge "a petty offense that usually calls for a token sentence." But, he added, "Acts of destroying the morale of the Army in training at Fort Sill constitute a very serious offense."

Of course, the indictment said nothing about destroying morale. In fact, the low morale at the base had an entirely different cause. It stemmed from the GIs' growing disgust with the war, from twelve-to-eighteen-hour workdays, from harsh punishments for minor offenses and from the arrogance of the brass.

Before being sentenced Maryann made a statement in the courtroom denouncing the war in Vietnam. She said there was no punishment the court could impose that would break the bond between civilians and GIs in their fight against the war. Key also asked permission to make a statement but was refused. "I'm not going to listen to any more of this," said Judge Bohanon.

Judge Bohanon gave Key and Maryann the maximum: he fined them each five hundred dollars and sentenced them to six months in a Federal penitentiary.

Outside the courtroom United Press International asked me to make a statement. I said: "Key and Maryann may have lowered the morale of the General, the Provost Marshal and the Criminal Investigation Division [CID], but they were raising the morale of the GIs."

The ACLU lawyers announced they would appeal, and Judge Bohanon set bail at $7,500, *cash* only, for each of the defendants. None of us had that kind of money, so Key and Maryann went to jail.

I was angry. The high appeal bond, set at fifteen times the fine, was obviously applied to restrict Key and Maryann's antiwar activities. In addition, it was a violation of the new bail law, which specifically prohibited the use of bail as punishment.

The day after the trial the brass moved the war resisters around to different units so it would be harder for us to communicate with each other. But there's always a way to get one-up on the brass if you work hard enough at it. We arranged to meet each night at a little house Dick Ilg had rented in anticipation of getting married should the seven-thousand-dollars insurance money ever come through.

September 1967 was a good month for us. Hundreds of GIs wrote and said they thought the union was a terrific idea. Now it was our job to get it off the ground. We finally decided that I would meet with eleven other GIs from eleven different military bases on Christmas Day to draw up a list of goals and to found the union. The meeting was to be held in New York City, where we thought we could get the maximum news coverage.

Deirdre returned to New York City two weeks after my court-martial, but we agreed to write to each other. The more time that went by, the more certain I was that I loved her.

It wasn't all work and no play at Ilg's house. We made up songs and sang them over mugs of beer. I remember one I particularly enjoyed. We sang it to the tune of "Join the NMU":

> Come, all you young soldiers,
> Good news to you I'll tell
> About a great new union
> That's really raising hell.
>
> The lifers are like bosses,
> They work us to the ground,
> But we will have the last word
> When we turn the guns around.

In the middle of September Dick Ilg's name came down on a levy for Vietnam. Ilg went to his commanding officer and said he wouldn't go.

Apparently because there had been so many courts-martial at Fort Sill, so much discussion about Key and Maryann languishing in jail, and so much fear over the possibility of another demonstration like the one that occurred on July 31, the Army decided to let the matter drop. One day a phone message came through from the Pentagon asking why Ilg wasn't with the contingent that was leaving. Ilg's battalion commander said that he was needed at Fort Sill, that he was too valuable a man to lose!

Ilg never did go to Vietnam. Instead he helped draw up the eight-point program that became the cornerstone of the American Servicemen's Union. The eight points are:

1. An End to the Saluting and Sir-ing of Officers

We believe this custom is degrading. It is a forced show of obedience designed to create an atmosphere of subservience. Some officers say the salute is a fraternal greeting, akin to the Masonic handgrip. That's bunk. When a GI salutes an officer he says, in effect, "Here I am, boss, ready to obey your commands," and when the officer returns the salute he's saying, "That's right, and don't you forget it." Other officers say it's a way for the GI to show respect. That's bunk too. Shows of respect are meaningless unless given voluntarily. And the Army doesn't even pretend to give a choice. It's the stockade for any GI who doesn't salute and say "sir."

2. Rank-and-File Control over Court-Martial Boards

At least on paper, civilians are guaranteed the right to trial by their peers. GIs forfeit that right the instant they enter the Army. This is wrong. Enlisted men should be judged by enlisted men, not by officers a thousand times removed from them in power and authority. Peer means equal. Yet officers have separate and far superior eating and living quarters, belong to clubs a GI can't even enter, wear uniforms that at once proclaim them as superior, sit in a chair behind a desk while the enlisted man stands at rigid attention, give orders the GI *has* to obey. No enlisted man of the rank of PFC or lower has *ever* sat on a court-martial board, despite the fact that more than 90 percent of those court-martialed are PFC or lower.

3. An End to Racism in the Armed Forces

The racism is cynical and it is deliberate. Its purpose is to divide enlisted men from one another in order to prevent unity in the fight against the brass. The Army is an expert practitioner of "Divide and conquer." And it is a fact that black and Spanish-speaking GIs are given the most dangerous assignments and suffer the highest casualty rates.

4. Federal Minimum Wages for All Enlisted Men

A GI is paid approximately twenty cents an hour while some Generals make upward of $50,000 a year. It is not right that the families of many enlisted men are forced onto welfare rolls while the families of officers trip off to the Riviera. Many officers sipping Daiquiris in Saigon officers' clubs make twenty times as much money as the GI whose life is on the line in the swamps and jungles. A man should be paid by work, not rank.

5. The Right of GIs to Collective Bargaining

It is impossible for Pentagon Generals and overfed congressmen to represent the interests of the enlisted man. It is the same as letting corporation executives determine how much a worker should earn. Until the GI has the right to bargain collectively, and therefore obtain some political and economic power, he will remain in virtual bondage. And the bargaining must apply to the whole spectrum of Army life.

6. The Right of Free Political Association

Unless the GI unquestioningly accepts everything the brass tell him to believe, he is a "subversive." The enlisted man has a mind of his own and should be allowed to use it. And, since *his* life is at stake, he, more than anyone else, has the right to organize and agitate against decisions that are not in his best interests. The brass organize and agitate among themselves for business and banking groups that want defense contracts or want to use enlisted men's lives to protect their far-flung financial investments.

7. The Election of Officers by Enlisted Men

GIs should not be led by a self-appointed caste of officers who represent the interests of the rich rather than the interests of the people. The only way to prevent servicemen from being sent to fight and die in battles for the rich is for officers to be elected by the men and to be subject to recall at any time. Anything less perpetuates the rule over the Armed Forces by a small clique of Generals whose main interests lie in strengthening the military caste system and serving the corporations for whom they will one day work.

8. The Right to Disobey Illegal and Immoral Orders

Orders must serve the needs of the people. The GI has a duty to disobey orders such as those that send him to die in that miserable, immoral war in Vietnam. It is the GI's life, he has only one life, and it is not right that he should sacrifice it just because some officer tells him to. Enlisted men, if organized, would have tremendous power. They could refuse to provide the sinew and muscle to fight the battles of flabby businessmen and arrogant brass hats.

"Suppose they gave a war and nobody came?"

CHAPTER IX   Toward the end of September 1967, with the platform I was going to present to the other GIs on Christmas Day pretty well worked out, I applied for a week's leave. I wanted to go to New York City and talk with people who had had experience organizing. I didn't expect to get the leave. The brass had become almost hysterically paranoid over the growing antiwar sentiment on base. They imagined I was responsible for the war resistance (they were) and began to react in typical fashion. Fifteen GIs, all of them in favor of the union, were transferred out of Fort Sill to bases as far away from each other—and me—as possible. Of course, all that this accomplished was to bring our message firsthand to fifteen additional bases.

I was very much surprised when my request for leave was granted. I took a plane to New York City, and the first person I talked with was Fayette Richardson. Richardson had been a paratrooper during World War II and had fought through both the Normandy and Ardennes campaigns. He won the Bronze Star at Normandy. This brave man, raised in a conservative small town in upper New York State, was the first ex-GI to speak out publicly against the war in Vietnam. He did it on Veterans Day, 1965, at a rally in Union Square.

Richardson was an active unionist and had been the editor of *Buffalo Labor Action*. He was interested in the idea of a union for GIs and agreed to write a handbook explaining why such an organization was needed. Thirty days later the *GI's Handbook on Military Injustice* was completed. Thanks to pro-union GIs throughout the world who were willing to defy the brass's ban of the handbook and distribute it to their buddies, Richardson's treatise enjoyed a large readership.

I also visited my friends from YAWF and NECLC and BAND. They were enthusiastic about the union and promised to promote it in their publications.

But the person I spent the most time with was Deirdre Griswold. We decided to get married almost as soon as we met again and six days later had our blood tests. We had made arrangements to be married the next day, the last day of my leave.

It wasn't to be. I developed severe abdominal pains and was taken to the hospital. The doctor said he didn't know what was the matter (it wasn't diagnosed as appendicitis until December), but he wired Fort Sill and told them I was in no condition to travel. The commanding officer thought it was a trick to extend my leave and ordered me to return immediately. When I arrived at the base I had a temperature of 105 and couldn't walk. I spent a week in the hospital receiving massive doses of penicillin. Then they sent me back to humping ammo.

Shortly after I was released from the hospital, Military Intelligence agents launched what came to be known as "The Great Fried-Chicken Hunt."

One of the eyewitnesses at my first court-martial had published an article that gave a lively description of the trial, the demonstration and evening we had all spent together afterward eating fried chicken. The author mentioned that he had been a sergeant. The story was picked up by Radio Hanoi and broadcast in Vietnam. When the brass got wind of this they ordered an investigation. Specifically, they wanted to find the sergeant who was hobnobbing with "subversives." It never occurred to the brass that he might have been a sergeant during World War II, which indeed was the case. They were sure they were on the trail of a traitor and they intended to flush him out.

The brass located a picture published in the left-wing brochure *Soldiers Against the War* showing a group of us eating chicken. Now, the brass reasoned, if they could only identify the people . . .

A pair of warrant officers confronted Paul Gaedtke.

"Look, Gaedtke, we want to know who that sergeant was."

"What sergeant?"

"The one who had the fried chicken with you and Stapp and the others."

"I don't remember his name."

The officers played their hole card. One pulled out the picture he had clipped from the brochure and said: "Either identify these people or you'll go to the stockade. Who's this man?"

"Eddie Oquendo."

"And this?"

"Ernie Weissman."

"And this?"

"Key Martin."

They made Gaedtke identify everyone in the picture. When he had finished, they still had not learned the name of the mysterious sergeant.

"Goddam it, Gaedtke, who was that sergeant?"

"I told you I don't know his name."

"Where was he when this picture was taken?"

"Can't you guess?"

"Don't play games, Gaedtke."

"He was the one who took the picture."

The brass never did crack the case, though they deserve an A for effort. They were still questioning people six months later.

On September 30, 1967, I was again invited to speak to students at the University of Oklahoma. This time I was able to make it. The meeting was sponsored jointly by SDS and the University of Oklahoma Committee to End the War in Vietnam. My topic was racism in the Army, so I had plenty to say. During my speech I noticed a man in the front row who somehow didn't belong. He was dressed in what he thought was college attire—madras shirt, Bermuda shorts, dark glasses and open sandals—but he looked so uncomfortable I was pretty sure he was a cop.

At the beginning of the question-and-answer period a civilian stood up in the middle of the room and said: "I think a lot of people here would be interested to know that the 501st Military Intelligence Group at Fort Hood has sent two agents to keep an eye on Private Stapp. Let's have a nice hand for the Military Intelligence agents from Fort Hood."

Everyone in the room began to laugh and clap his hands.

"Come on, folks," the man continued. "Let's *really* hear it for the Military Intelligence agents from Fort Hood."

This time the applause was thunderous.

When the noise subsided the man said: "In the best traditions of Military Intelligence, they didn't cheer for themselves. But at least take a bow, won't you, fellows?"

The agent in the madras shirt and Bermuda shorts got up and left. He was followed by another man more soberly attired. The civilian (a former Military Intelligence agent himself) who had called attention to the pair told me that he had worked with them at Fort Hood and that their clumsiness as sleuths had earned them a nickname—the Keystone Cops. Army pamphlet 360-17, a recruiting manual for military police, describes these undercover agents as follows: "Army investigating agents are hard at work around the world. From the foggy streets of London, the teeming byways of Asian cities, to the sidewalks of New York and San Francisco. A career in this corps of investigators is a career in police work with the Free World as a beat."

Each day Deirdre and I were on the phone trying to arrange a time when we could be married. Whenever she was able to get away, I was on duty. Finally, a month after our first attempt, she flew to Oklahoma and we did it.

Dick Wheaton was our witness and he drove us into Lawton. Our first stop was the county clerk's office to pick up a license. Then it was on to a justice of the peace to complete the formalities. Outside, however, were three Military Intelligence agents who had followed Wheaton's car from the base. It wasn't long before we had shaken our tails.

The next morning, while relaxing in the tub, we opened the *Daily Oklahoman* and caught a headline: "War Protester Weds Editor." For an instant I thought there must be an antiwar GI at Fort Sill whom I hadn't heard about. I had forgotten Deirdre was an editor, too.

We had each other for only three days. But we knew we would be together at Christmas, when I was due for another week's leave, and, anyway, I would be out of the Army for good in May. We had a last laugh together before Deirdre boarded the plane for New York. Asked by the *Daily Oklahoman* to comment on our marriage, the head of Military Intelligence said, "Like a Rockefeller marrying a duPont, it's a political merger."

It was flattering to know that the brass thought our political power comparable to that of the super-rich.

During October 1967 officer morale at Fort Sill dipped to a new low. Although the newspapers hushed up the story, word leaked out that the 198th Light Infantry Brigade at Fort Hood, Texas, had rebeled and leveled large sections of the base, causing more than $150,000 damage. A lieutenant was killed in the fighting and grenades had been thrown into the officers' club.

What was happening at Fort Sill was just as disheartening to the brass. Atrocity reports by returned combat veterans had brought many GIs close to refusing to obey orders sending them to Vietnam. Hundreds of these eyewitness accounts circulated around the base. Some of the ones I heard from returned veterans were: four prisoners, their bodies strapped together with baling wire, thrown from a U.S. helicopter; a concentration camp so overcrowded that a hundred NLF prisoners were executed to make more room; tubes forced down the noses of prisoners with water poured in to drown them; a fifteen-year-old Vietnamese girl gang-raped by three sergeants; a Green Beret captain who employed castration to force confessions.

There were more, many more, but one doesn't have the heart or the stomach to recount them all. There were also the descriptions of how the Vietnamese got their revenge: the NLF, hiding in ambush in trees and bushes, let a five-hundred-man search-and-destroy mission pass through so they could open fire on the officers bringing up the rear; a ten-year-old Vietnamese girl giving a sergeant a Coca-Cola that eventually killed him because it was mixed with battery acid; a "pacified" seventy-year-old farmer caught attempting to ambush a survey team by planting a mine in the road.

Accounts like these shocked many GIs into realizing that virtually the entire Vietnamese people was fighting to drive out the U.S. troops.

Finally, in November, the brass could no longer ignore

the increasing hostility of the GIs. They decided to conduct their own version of a war-crimes tribunal. Hearings were held at post headquarters—McNair Hall—and their stated purpose was to uncover war crimes in Vietnam. Their real purpose was to smoke out the Vietnam veterans who had talked about war atrocities.

GIs are not as stupid as the brass think. More than a hundred witnesses were called and not one divulged any names. To do so would have been to subject the veterans who had related the stories to certain harassment and probable punishment.

Dick Wheaton was called twice. Each time he refused to talk, saying that what he had heard was meant for his ears alone.

I was called once. Here's the way it went:

"Private Stapp, if we're to correct the things the men are complaining about we need documentation. We need names. Who do we look to?"

"Look to yourselves. The great crimes of war aren't committed by privates and corporals, but by majors and colonels and generals like yourselves."

One GI, short, thin, with glasses and a mild manner, politely asked: "Colonel, is this microphone live?"

"It is, son."

"Hi, Mom!"

The last GI to testify had recently come back from Vietnam. "I don't know anything about what's been brought up here," he said, "but I do remember seeing people being buried alive."

The brass possess a certain *chutzpah*. In the report they sent to Washington when the hearings ended they said: "Despite a thorough and comprehensive investigation, not a scintilla of evidence was uncovered to indicate war crimes."

On November 12, 1967, I was called to the office of

Colonel Lenhart, head of G-2 Post Intelligence. Lenhart fancied himself a humorist; he had a sign on his desk that read, "My work is so secret even I don't know what I'm doing."

The paper Lenhart wanted me to sign wasn't funny at all. It stated: "I hereby waive my rights to a Field Board Hearing under Army Regulation 604-10. I will accept whatever discharge is authorized under AR 604-10, knowing that a less than honorable discharge can cause substantial prejudice against me in civilian life."

AR 604-10 is known as a national security discharge, and for a moment I thought Lenhart was kidding. Certainly he didn't think I was going to sign. But he did.

"Save us a lot of trouble, Stapp. Then you can join that pretty wife of yours."

I did a fast burn. I knew it wasn't the security of the United States they were worried about. They were afraid that the organization I was helping to build was a threat to *their* security. The brass were scared that a union of servicemen would undermine everything they glory in—the privilege and power and position, the right to unquestioned obedience, the smug satisfaction derived from a snappy salute and above all the big pay differential and the thousand material advantages they enjoy in contrast to the wretched living conditions and rotten pay the GIs receive.

All of a sudden I wanted to laugh. Here was a Colonel, part and parcel of the mightiest military machine on earth, and he was worried that a few hundred angry GIs could just possibly topple him off his high and mighty perch.

I tossed Lenhart's piece of paper into the waste basket and demanded a Field Board Hearing.

Two days later I was informed that the hearing would be held on January 4.

CHAPTER X On Christmas morning, 1967, the American Servicemen's Union was officially founded. Fourteen of us, each from a different base but each for the same reasons, agreed to the union's eight-point program. There were two more GIs present at the meeting than had been originally planned. I was elected chairman of the union.

We already had hundreds of GIs willing to join, but it was decided not to accept formal membership yet. We were gathering an editorial and technical staff for a newspaper that would be the organizing tool of the union. Each of the fourteen GIs at the meeting was to return to his base and test the union's program and impact through practice.

At first we had intended to start the union with a fanfare of publicity but now decided to do it quietly. At every Army base in America the brass had posted the following warning: "Military personnel will not participate in any activity having to do with creating a union for enlisted men."

As was often the case, the brass had unwittingly done us a favor. Although many GIs knew of our activities, the majority did not. The brass gave us the kind of publicity we needed without our having to announce our plans in the commercial press.

The meeting in New York ended in time for Deirdre and

me to catch a bus to my parents' home in Pennsylvania for Christmas dinner. Deirdre had participated in a strike to organize Brooklyn hospitals, and on the way to Pennsylvania we discussed some suggestions she had on how to organize members for the ASU.

My mother had prepared a turkey dinner, but none of us got a chance to enjoy it. Everyone was too busy rushing me to the hospital. I had appendicitis. Luckily Dr. Blakemore, our next-door neighbor, was a surgeon. He operated at once. The appendix had burst and I had peritonitis.

On New Year's Day, when my leave ended, I was still being fed intravenously and had two tubes in the incision. Dr. Blakemore phoned Fort Sill and told them he would not let me be moved. First the brass called the hospital to make sure I was really sick, then they called Dr. Blakemore and said that since they had to foot the bill they wanted me moved to Valley Forge Veterans' Hospital, twenty miles away, where it would cost the Army less. Reluctantly Dr. Blakemore agreed.

Two sergeants came the next day and carried me out of the hospital on a stretcher. With the tubes still in my side, I was put in an ambulance and driven to the Fort Dix Hospital, where there is an airfield, not to the hospital at Valley Forge.

Deirdre, after a dozen phone calls, finally found out where I was and with a friend drove immediately to Fort Dix. She located my room and, since it was visiting hours, started to walk in. A nurse hurried over to intercept her: "You can't visit this man; the officer of the day said he was to have no visitors."

When Deirdre persisted, two burly orderlies came to stand in front of the door with their arms folded. Deirdre sat down in the hallway and said she wouldn't move until they let her see me. After a long wait she was allowed in the room for five minutes. The next day they gave her an hour and the day after that they put me on a Medivac plane for Fort Sill.

It was a World War II cargo plane and it made more than fifteen stops to let sick passengers on and off. It took fifty-six hours to get to Fort Sill. It was winter and every time the door opened the temperature went down to about 20 degrees. The only food I had been allowed at the hospital was tea and soup, but the nurse on the plane offered me a ham sandwich. When I told her I was on a liquid diet she found some milk. In my semidelirium I imagined that the brass were trying to kill me, but the saner part of my mind said that after all this was the Army, they always did things this way. If there was a cumbersome, blundering, irrational method of doing something, the Army could be counted on to ferret it out. And I knew the Army's aim was rational enough: to get me back to Fort Sill, dead or alive, in time for the Field Board Hearing.

There were TV cameras at the airport when we landed and some of my friends watched me being taken off the plane. They hurried over to the hospital and were there to greet me when I arrived.

I was in the hospital four weeks. The Field Board Hearing was postponed week by week. It was held the day I came out.

I had a lot of visitors in the hospital and plenty of time to catch up on my letter-writing. One of the people I had written to earlier was Dick Perrin, who had been thrown in solitary for fifteen days for being in Lawton without a pass. Perrin was supposed to be in Germany, but each time I wrote to him my letters were returned. I learned the reason one night while watching television. The program originated in Paris and was about a group of American deserters who had formed an organization they called RITA (Resistance Inside The Army). Right in the middle of the screen, looking exactly as he had the day they shipped him out, was Dick Perrin. He was with Stokely Carmichael and Terry Klug (another deserter, the son of a United Nations official, and an American Servicemen's Union member). Perrin and Klug had gone AWOL at the same time and were instrumental in forming RITA. I wrote to Perrin that night and we have corresponded ever since.

I also kept in touch with Fayette Richardson in New York, since the two of us had made arrangements to publish our newspaper for servicemen. On the West Coast, Bill Callison had been putting out a newspaper called *The Bond* (the title referred to the bond between antiwar civilians and antiwar GIs), but he was arrested for draft resistance and had to give it up. A number of antiwar groups had asked Callison to let them use *The Bond*'s name, but he decided to give it to Richardson and me along with his one-thousand-name mailing list.

Richardson, Bill Smith and I got *The Bond* rolling. Richardson did the technical work in New York, I wrote a number of articles from my hospital bed and Bill Smith, who had just returned from Vietnam, wrote about his war experiences. Smith is still Vietnam editor of *The Bond*. Here's a sample of what he wrote for our first issue:

> In Vietnam the worst non-combat jobs the Pentagon IBM machines can shove you into are those connected to Army transportation. The stevedores of this program labor the hardest and in many cases find themselves in the most dangerous positions.
>
> Besides regular company details, my outfit averaged ten to twelve hours a day unloading Johnson's napalm. And if we didn't meet the quota set by our commanding officer, we worked until he was satisfied, sometimes up to seventeen hours a day.
>
> If you are unloading in the Delta or on any of the mainland

rivers, your life expectancy can be cut to seconds. Commanding officer, however, doesn't worry about this. He does his work from a sandbagged headquarters more than a mile away, and he knows that patriotic draft boards can replace you.

Before my company left for operations further north at Duc Phu and Chu Lai, a struggle developed at our home base in Cam Ranh Bay that gave me my first lesson on the power of unions.

The men in my platoon had to work in other company areas on the same days we sweated for twelve hours in the hatches of rat-infested merchant vessels. We decided to protest. A group of us drew up a list of grievances and then, led by two Sp/4's, marched to the orderly tent and assumed the traditional parade-rest.

The CO talked to us and, after giving his reasons for the extra work, threatened us with a charge of mutiny (which can bring a death sentence). But we stood firm and read the list of grievances.

There were seventy-five of us and mutiny charges against that many GIs would have made front pages. The CO continued to talk tough but the next day the extra duty we had been pulling ended.

The Bond now has more than 75,000 readers, and Bill Smith receives dozens of letters each week. GIs know he tells it like it is. But Smith isn't the kind of guy who wants only to sit and write about the past. He is one of the union's most successful organizers.

The first issue of the new *Bond* was off the press on January 30, 1968, just in time to be flown to Fort Sill for distribution at my Field Board Hearing.

A piece of news that heartened me during my stay in the hospital came from Bloomington, Indiana, where SDS was holding its national conference. SDS unanimously adopted a resolution of support for the American Servicemen's Union and called for demonstrations against my upcoming Field Board Hearing. Protests were held in New York City, Philadelphia, Cleveland and Milwaukee.

Many things happened while I was in the hospital, among them Paul Gaedtke's second trip to the stockade. Because of his antiwar activities Gaedtke was continually being assigned the heaviest and dirtiest jobs the brass could find. So when a sergeant was put in charge of retrieving thousands of feet of cable lying in a field, he ordered Gaedtke and two other GIs to wind it on twelve-foot-high spools. It was a job that would take four days and the weather was freezing and windy. After several hours the three GIs thought their hands and feet would fall off. But Gaedtke noticed a jeep parked nearby and got an idea. He fastened the end of the cable to the jeep and let the jeep do the work for them. Not only were they able to keep warm but the idea worked so well it was obvious they would finish the job in one day. Then the sergeant came back from a two-hour coffee break.

"What the hell are you doing?" he shouted.

"We've found a more efficient way," Gaedtke told him.

"I don't want no fuckin' efficiency. You unwind that cable and start over."

That's when Gaedtke hit him in the mouth.

Paul was feeling pretty cocky when he went into the stockade. He managed to smuggle in a dozen copies of the *GI's Handbook on Military Injustice,* thanks to the fact that the stockade guard who frisked him was a GI who had agreed to join the union. The handbook, written by Fayette Richardson, was strong stuff and the prisoners loved it.

It took the brass a week to find out about the handbook and then they threw Gaedtke into a basement cell with a drug addict who had gone crazy because he couldn't get a fix. The addict thought Gaedtke had been put into his cell to beat him up. Gaedtke spent twenty-three days with the man, and neither slept very well because of fear that one would attack if the other dozed off.

An incident occurred during Gaedtke's stay in the stockade that made him aware of the growing solidarity between black and white GIs. He was on a work gang cutting down brush. The armed guard who watched over the work gang wouldn't allow anyone to go off alone to urinate. It was too risky. There had been too many escapes that way. If a prisoner wanted to go, the guard asked the other men if they would accompany him. One day a black prisoner requested permission, and when the guard asked the others to go along, one fellow refused. So nobody went, and the black prisoner had to hold it in for three hours until they got back to the latrine.

That evening the prisoners conducted a trial. It wasn't like a court-martial, because the accused was tried by a jury of his peers. He was found guilty of prejudice and unfair treatment to a fellow prisoner. Later that night he fell down and broke his leg.

CHAPTER XI   A Field Board Hearing is neither a trial nor a court-martial. It is supposed to be an impartial hearing in front of a board of experts and it has no power to sentence or fine. In my case it was held to determine whether I was a national security risk, and if the board so found, I would be given an undesirable discharge. At a Field Board Hearing the defendant is not called the accused but the respondent. Instead of a judge there is a president of the board. Instead of a prosecutor there is an attorney-adviser.

I was allowed two lawyers—one from the Judge Advocate Corps, Captain James McNutt, who did a pretty good job on the whole, and one of my own choosing, Michael Kennedy of the NECLC. Kennedy, a brilliant guy, has for years been intensely interested in defending civil liberties. With my case he was particularly interested in shedding light on the irregular and unconstitutional proceedings of Field Board Hearings. Time and again he objected when evidence was introduced without proper foundation and when constitutional guarantees were violated. But the president of the board overruled nineteen out of every twenty objections he made.

One violation of my rights was that the board had before

it an "incriminating" 37-page document, which neither my attorneys nor I were allowed to see. Nor were we given any idea of what the document contained or why it was incriminating. We were not even permitted to be present at the final meeting of the board when its findings and recommendations were made. I do have the 283-page transcript of the public part of the hearing. The president of the board's last comment was: "All personnel present are reminded that the findings and recommendations are classified information not to be made public or to be divulged to the individual concerned or to his counsel."

Spectators were allowed at the public part of the hearing and Deirdre came. GIs were warned to stay away, but one of them, Robert LeMay, a Vietnam veteran and later a national leader in the American Servicemen's Union, pushed his way past the MPs and stayed for the entire hearing.

The hearing began on January 31, 1968, and the first order of business was to inform me of my rights and their limitations: "It is your responsibility to refute, rebut or raise doubt as to the credibility, accuracy or adequacy of the allegations which have been presented by the government as reflecting against you."

In other words, I was guilty until I could prove myself innocent. Michael Kennedy jumped up to object: "The United States Court of Military Appeals and the Congress of the United States do not have the power, by themselves, to change the Fifth Amendment, which quite clearly reads that you are innocent until proven guilty."

Kennedy's objection was overruled and the president of the board proceeded to read the charges against me: (1) that I had a close, continuing and sympathetic association with the Communist party; (2) that I had been in close, continuing and sympathetic association with Maryann Weissman; and (3) that I was a risk to national security.

The first charge was silly, though understandable considering the Army's abysmal ignorance of what constitutes a Communist. On the West Coast there is a tiny splinter group (I believe they have four members) that broke away from the Communist party several years ago and that calls itself "The Communist Party of the United States." They had put out a poster two years before that I had purchased for a dollar. When the brass broke open my foot locker they found a receipt for that dollar. The receipt was the Army's only evidence of my "close, continuing and sympathetic association with the Communist party."

As for the charge that I was closely associated with Maryann Weissman, I was proud to affirm it.

Michael Kennedy and all the witnesses, both my own and the Army's, proved to the satisfaction of any person in his right mind that the third charge, which strongly implied that I was involved in espionage, was hogwash. Even Colonel Price testified that I never had access to classified material and that I had neither wanted nor been given a security clearance.

However, there was much more involved in this accusation than the question of security clearance. I had learned, along with every other American schoolchild, that we lived in "one nation, indivisible," and had accepted that concept as a child. But as I got older and learned some things about history and observed the relationships among groups of people I began to realize that the "indivisible nation" of my young ideals had always been an illusion—indeed, a hoax. The founding fathers, it turned out, were slave-owners, aristocrats who had separated themselves from the great majority of the American people just as surely as the millionaires of today seclude themselves at Newport and Palm Beach while their minions go scurrying around the world in search of new fortunes and cheap native labor.

To the brass who would judge me, they and their kind were the "nation"—the 2 or 3 percent of the American people who were the Generals, the bankers, the owners of industry, the big-time politicians. It was *their* lives and *their* wealth that had to be made secure. They didn't give a damn about the security of the other 195 million of us, of the half million men fighting in the jungles of Vietnam, or the vast numbers just managing to keep their financial heads above water, to whom one major illness means destitution, or the millions of black Americans struggling for dignity in the slums.

The American way of life was supposed to be made up of equal parts of free enterprise and hard work, but if Grandpa was free enough with his enterprise, his descendants would never see a day of hard work. For the Rockefellers, the duPonts, the Whitneys, the Mellons and others whose ancestors swindled their way to huge fortunes capitalism is a fine form of government. But the welfare mother, scraping along on Nixon's guaranteed sixteen-hundred a year and observing the duPonts raking in hundreds of millions while lolling on yachts on the Delaware River, might think that she works harder for her money than the rich do for theirs. Something is terribly wrong with a system that permits a few, because of the accident of birth, to have so much while many millions have so little.

The brass are well aware of the deep divisions in this "indivisible nation." Each time they walk into an officers' club, or bark out an order, or send a GI to a stockade, where the officer will never go no matter how serious his crime, or negotiate a multibillion-dollar defense contract, or force a GI to storm a hill in Vietnam—on all these occasions and more the brass are aware of the division. They are also aware that on their side of the dividing line is a very small minority of the people. On the other side are the 97 percent who exist to serve them.

I had talked about these inequities. And the brass knew that some people were listening. That's what made me a risk to "national" security.

The first four Government witnesses called to testify at my Field Board Hearing didn't do much to advance the Army's case. The first was Paul Gaedtke. The brass must have thought that after twenty-three days in the "rabbit room" (so named because the only food served was bread and lettuce) he had been sufficiently softened to see the error of his ways.

"Specialist Gaedtke," said the attorney-adviser, "are you familiar with the fact that Private Stapp had an apartment in Lawton?"

"Yes, sir, I am."

"Did you ever visit that apartment?"

"Yes."

"How many times were you there?"

"I couldn't count them."

"Quite a few times?"

"Maybe a thousand."

"A thousand times? That's quite a lot, isn't it?"

"Not really. You see, Private Stapp and I rented that apartment together. I lived there."

"I see. Did you and Private Stapp ever discuss political ideologies?"

"Oh, yes."

"Did you discuss any of the publications Private Stapp had?"

"Yes, we did."

"Do you recall the names of any of these publications?"

"Well, one was *Life* magazine."

At this point Captain McNutt, my military counsel, intervened with the objection that any reference to literature was a violation of the First Amendment. His objection was overruled.

"What other publications did Private Stapp have?"

"Time. U.S. News & World Report. Esquire."

"Did he have any publications which you used to discuss the Marxist or Communist line?"

"We talked about the Bible quite a bit."

Gaedtke was excused and taken back to the stockade. As he passed where I was sitting he gave me a clenched fist salute.

Dick Ilg was the second Government witness. At his secret court-martial in 1967 he had been scared and had given the answers the Army wanted. Naturally they thought he would fold again, but it was a different Dick Ilg this time.

"Do you know whether Private Stapp ever contributed money to the Communist party?"

"I have no knowledge of anything like that."

"Didn't he show you a receipt he had received from the Communist party?"

"No, sir, he did not."

"Were there any publications that Private Stapp had?"

"I don't understand the question."

"I think it's pretty clear. Did Private Stapp have any publications?"

"Yes, he had many publications."

"Name some of them."

"He had a few TMs and FMs."

"What?"

"Training Manuals and Field Manuals. They were passed out during basic training."

"Did he have a publication called the *Petitioner?*"

"Not that I know of."

"Did he have *I. F. Stone's Weekly?*"

"I have seen that publication."

"Anything entitled *Ramparts?*"

"I believe so. I might add that I saw one on the Battalion Adjutant's desk at Fort Chaffee, Arkansas. The same publication."

After more than twenty pages of testimony Ilg was unshaken and the attorney-adviser lost his cool. He demanded that his own witness be declared hostile so he could cross-examine him. Captain McNutt objected, and the board, composed of two lieutenants, one captain, three majors and three Colonels, sustained the objection. Captain McNutt was unable to conceal his surprise.

Ilg was dismissed, and the next witness to roll onto the stand was Larry LaFrance, a detective in the Lawton police department. LaFrance testified that he had been assigned to keep an eye on Maryann Weissman from June 4 to July 27, 1967. The attorney-adviser asked how many times he had seen Maryann and me together. LaFrance replied, "Once."

I had been with Maryann dozens of times during that period and we had never tried to conceal our meetings.

Lawton detective Loy Bean was the Army's fourth witness. Bean had also been assigned to follow Maryann, and at first he said he had seen us together two or three times a week. Under cross-examination he reduced this to three times in all.

The attorney-adviser realized he wasn't doing so well and decided to wheel out his big gun. He called to the stand Mrs. Helen Gittings, who described herself as "a research analyst for the House Un-American Activities Committee." Mrs. Gittings said she had been employed by HUAC for more than twenty years. Her function was to back up the Army's contention that Maryann Weissman had been a member of the Socialist Workers party from 1959 to 1963 and after that had joined the Workers World party. Mrs. Gittings testified that HUAC considered these organizations subversive.

Michael Kennedy rose to object: "The United States Army is potentially in the peculiar position of aligning itself with one of the most notorious witch-hunting organizations, one of the most un-American organizations in the United States itself, and that is the House Un-American Activities Committee. I think the United States Army would be doing itself a grave disservice if it disinterred the ugly head of Joe McCarthy again."

Of course the board disagreed with Kennedy's opinion of HUAC. Mrs. Gittings was treated with the greatest deference, even when she refused to answer most of Kennedy's questions on the grounds of a security privilege.

"What you are invoking, madam, so that we may all be clear, is a security privilege of one sort or another. Is that it?"

"You may define it as you wish."

"Well, is that it or not?"

"I would define it as a separation of power. I can think of lots of reasons, but I am invoking the privilege of not discussing it."

"The separation of the power of the House Un-American Activities Committee from democracy. Isn't that the separation of power you're talking about?"

Mrs. Gittings didn't answer. Michael Kennedy wasn't going to let her off easy.

"Mrs. Gittings, I take it that you have been instructed by somebody in the House Un-American Activities Committee that you are under an obligation not to divulge how reports such as Government Exhibit Number 20 [the one purporting to prove that Maryann had belonged to 'subversive' organizations] are prepared."

"Now you are talking about internal instructions and I am not speaking on that subject today."

Kennedy appealed to the president of the board: "I ask you to instruct the witness to answer the question."

The president answered: "Let me clarify the position I'm in. I can only request. I have no power to enforce. I will ask her to do what she considers—"

The attorney-adviser interrupted: "If the court please, this witness has received instructions from her superiors. Those instructions she must follow."

Kennedy responded angrily: "This is the problem, Mr. President. A witness is allowed to come into a hearing where my client faces an undesirable discharge from the Army; faces the loss of all the rights that have accrued to him while in the Army and to which he is entitled. He faces, potentially at least, the social opprobrium, the difficulty in finding employment. And the Government in attempting to establish that Private Stapp should be punished in this fashion brings in the rankest form of lies and hearsay. The Government brings them in by a person who probably had nothing to do with the preparation of the reports, and when I try to cross-examine the person to find out whether the documents are true, or even what they purport to be since defense is not allowed to read them, the witness, with the help of the attorney-adviser, invokes a privilege of one sort or another claiming that these are matters into which I cannot inquire. I object. I protest. This defies not only the human rights of everyone in any country in the world, but it defies the First, Fourth, Fifth, Sixth, Ninth and Tenth Amendments of the United States Constitution."

Kennedy's plea was disregarded and Mrs. Gittings was

told she didn't have to answer questions. Kennedy dismissed her from the stand with "Give my regards to the HUAC witch-hunters."

The next six Government witnesses were friends of mine. The attorney-adviser was determined to prove that I kept revolutionary literature. But no GI was going to help the brass. I have since seen countless examples in which enlisted men who didn't even know the accused would not even consider testifying against a fellow GI. The attorney-adviser was wasting his time.

Then the "incriminating" 37-page document was introduced into evidence. My lawyers were informed that they couldn't read it, nor would they be told of its contents. Michael Kennedy was near the end of his patience: "I cite what I believe to be the supreme law of the land, and that is the United States Constitution, namely the Sixth Amendment thereof, which guarantees to all persons the right to confront their accusers and to cross-examine them. I also cite the Fifth Amendment, which requires due process before one is deprived of life, liberty and whatever else. And certainly the liberties of Stapp and the rights of Stapp will be deprived if you undesirably discharge him from the United States Army. I know of no authority cited by the attorney-adviser that is higher than the Constitution of the United States, unless he is giving allegiance to some higher law than I know of. I consider this of such significance, Mr. President, that I request that the members of the board be polled on the issue."

The members of the board were polled and they ruled that the secret document would remain secret.

I thought my hearing was probably the most unfair in recorded history. Later I learned there was nothing unusual about it at all. One of the most important functions the American Servicemen's Union would begin to perform was to help provide free legal counsel for GIs facing courts-martial.

The hearing recessed for lunch and Deirdre and I were immediately surrounded by reporters from as far away as New York and Los Angeles. Deirdre had brought copies of our first issue of *The Bond* and she gave one to each newsman. One of the local reporters handed his copy to Colonel Lenhart, the same Colonel Lenhart, head of G-2 Post Intelligence, who had asked me to sign a paper waiving my right to a hearing. Lenhart did not look happy as he began to read *The Bond*.

On the front page was my picture, and right beside it was a picture of General Earle G. Wheeler, Chairman of the Joint Chiefs of Staff.

The caption under my picture read: "He demands that servicemen have rights. He says you must receive higher pay, that you must have a voice in the conditions under which you work and that there must be racial equality. He says that enlisted men must have seats on court-martial boards and that you should elect your own officers, that you must have all the rights of free men including the right to refuse illegal orders to fight an illegal war—like the one in Vietnam—and that the only way to get these rights is to organize a union of rank-and-file GIs."

The caption under Wheeler's picture read: "He speaks for the power structure. He says you do as you're told no matter what it is. If he orders you to go to Vietnam and get killed, you aren't supposed to ask questions. It's just your job to die for important people like him. He says, I and the people that count give the orders and you just do what you're told and shut up about it and say 'sir' when you're talking to an officer."

The first issue of *The Bond* also carried a full page of letters the union had received. I'll quote a few:

Your example has inspired us to openly declare ourselves against the war in Vietnam. We have seen too many of our buddies die just so Big Business can continue making a fast buck. We pledge ourselves to work for your union's demands. [Signed by PFCs Maury Knutson, Thomas Wake and Andrew Holloway—all from Fort Benning.]

Through lectures and Battle Glory films, the brass think they can remold my beliefs into theirs. It won't work. In January I receive my orders to go to Vietnam. I will refuse them. [Signed by PFC Raymond Benish, Fort Sam Houston.]

I just got your name from the *Berkeley Barb*, and I would like to receive your newspaper, *The Bond*. I am in the midst of deciding whether to go into the Army and fuck them up from within or to move to another country. [From a student, John Arrington.]

The brass prefer to ignore this kind of dissent, just as they publicly ignore the 190,000 desertions in 1967–68.

But the dissent is not going to go away. More and more young men—and ever-growing numbers of their elders—are beginning to turn away in revulsion from a system that places their lives in forfeit to a policy that can and will change, depending on the whims of the military engineers in the Pentagon. A decision goes down that a certain hill must be taken, that a certain camp must be defended—"at whatever cost." To the working stiffs doing the actual fighting that cost may well be an arm or a leg, or life itself. "The supreme sacrifice" is a noble-sounding phrase for a Fourth of July speech, but its reality is mud and death and a military mortuary where they scrape the blood off your dogtags so they can read your name, and parents, too old to bear any more sons, and young wives suddenly become widows, and children orphans, with nothing left of a young father but a few pieces of paper, a crumbling uniform and a couple of dusty medals.

So the battle is fought, the necessary hill is taken, or the necessary camp defended. The human machines in the Pentagon think it over for a week or so, long enough for the telegrams to be sent to the States, long enough for the survivors to be spooned onto stretchers and taken to hospitals, long enough for the flag to be raised and the press to gloat, long enough for everyone to inhale the scent of victory.

Then the decision is made that the hill is no longer necessary, or the camp really wasn't that vital after all; so the soldiers troop back down the winding path to the plain below, or clean their supplies out of their bunkers and load them onto waiting trucks. They leave. The men they fought glide silently out of hiding, tend their wounded, bury their dead, retake the hill, occupy the abandoned camp. Everything in that spot is now the same as it was before.

But not the same. Lives have been lost, and in this game called war there is no recovery of losses. Young men, their childhood barely ended, are dead. Dead is a long time. Dead means no more college, no medical school, no laboratory where you would serve mankind, no high school sweetheart that you planned to marry, no children to carry on your name. For the young, death is a guillotine.

What epitaph shall we give all those young dead? "I died, and then they changed their minds"—how about that?

How long must the young go on dying at the pleasure of others? How long must they pay with their blood for the ambitions of Generals and the greed of corporations? Or is the day coming when they will turn and say, "If you want this war, you go and fight it. If it means that much to you, you make that sacrifice you so grandly call 'supreme.'"

CHAPTER XII   After the noon recess the Army announced it had concluded its case. Now it was Michael Kennedy's turn and he called Melvin Hoit, a friend of mine who was later sentenced to three years in Leavenworth for disobeying an officer's order.

"Did Private Stapp ever indicate to you," Kennedy asked, "that he had or has a close, continuing and sympathetic relationship with the Communist party?"

"No, sir."

"Are you aware of any information to indicate that Private Stapp is a risk to the security of the United States Army or the United States Government?"

"No, sir."

"Do you believe Private Stapp is a loyal soldier?"

"Yes, sir. I believe he is very concerned with soldiers' rights and with upholding the Constitution of the United States within the Army."

Kennedy said he had no further questions, but before Hoit could step down, one of the board members began to interrogate him.

"Specialist Hoit, I would be interested to know your definition of a loyal soldier?"

"I believe a loyal soldier would honor the oath he took at

induction, which says he will defend the Constitution."

"Specialist Hoit, correct me if I'm wrong. Doesn't that oath also say he will obey his superiors? Isn't that part of being a loyal soldier?"

"I believe, sir, that a soldier must obey his superiors if he believes he's been given a legal order. The soldier has a right and a duty to disobey illegal orders."

"Do you believe a loyal soldier supports the United States Government?"

"I would qualify that, sir. I would say a loyal soldier supports the United States Constitution."

"In other words, you believe there is a dividing line. If the United States Government is not complying with the United States Constitution, you believe the loyal soldier should choose the Constitution. Is that correct?"

"Yes, sir."

"Do you believe that Private Stapp supports the United States Constitution?"

"I do, sir. Definitely."

"Do you think that Private Stapp supports the United States Government?"

"I would say that he disagrees with some of the Government's policies, as all soldiers do."

"Would Private Stapp obey an order from the United States Government if that order went against what he believes the Constitution says?"

"You would have to ask Private Stapp. I'm not qualified to speak for him."

"Yet you're qualified to say that he's a loyal soldier?"

"Yes, sir."

"Can I have an opinion on the other part too?"

"You're asking me what Private Stapp would do. I don't think I can answer that question."

Hoit was dismissed and Kennedy proceeded to call a half-dozen of my friends to the witness stand. Among them was Dick Wheaton. Wheaton had been warned before he testified that he could not invoke Article 31 of the Uniform Code of Military Justice, that article being the military equivalent of the constitutional protection against self-incrimination. Unbelievably, the brass told him that if he invoked Article 31, they would consider him a Communist. They could have saved their breath. Wheaton *wanted* to testify. And so did the others. They were not going to be scared off by threats and intimidation. With all the witnesses called in my behalf, the board hammered away on two points: my political views; my position on violence. What "subversive" ideas was I expounding? they demanded to know. Some of those who testified were reluctant to confide to the brass hats what I had been saying, so I'll say it now.

I said that I believed in true democracy, not the sham that exists in the United States, where the amount of money the individual has at his disposal determines whether he'll be elected or not. I said that the people were being exploited economically and that the workers should own the means of production and should have control over their own lives. Needless to say, this is not the way things are in this country, where power is concentrated in the hands of the few, who are allowed to enrich themselves at the expense of the others. I said that I was against imperialist wars such as the United States' war against Vietnam, that I was against such actions as the United States' intervention in Santo Domingo, the United States' occupation of Guantanamo Bay and the ruthless CIA meddling in Guatemala in 1954.

Regarding violence, I said that it should not be used until *all* peaceful means of transition to a people's democracy are exhausted, but when they are, and when the ruling class continues to set its face against the will of the majority, and particularly when it uses violence, then violence is the correct and proper and only response. I said I didn't believe in government by *coup d'état,* such as the small military junta that seized power in Greece, or Franco in Spain, or Batista in Cuba. I said that a majority of the people must favor a violent overthrow of the government, and that violence must be the people's *only* recourse before it could be condoned.

Other board members wanted to know how many times I had been with the dangerous Maryann Weissman. But their greatest preoccupation of all was the subject of violence. They were just horrified, these professional killers, these votaries of violence, to think that we, their pupils, would talk about the violence of the state against the poor, the voiceless, the minorities. And that we should even consider violence under certain circumstances and at some time in the future—well, that was appalling. But worst of all was our rejection of the one violence they most approved—the war in Vietnam. To be violent on their terms was fine. To suggest it might be acceptable on any other terms was wicked. And to refuse it in the name of decency and justice was simply unthinkable.

Late in the afternoon, with everyone tired and wanting to be done with it all, Michael Kennedy made his summation:

"If you decide to undesirably discharge Private Stapp from the United States Army, he will lose the GI Bill of Rights, which amounts to a large amount of money; he will lose his accrued leave, which can also be a large sum of money; he will lose Federal employment opportunities and the preferences given to soldiers; and he will lose a myriad other benefits—but more important for you, the United States Army in general and you people in particular will have gotten into the witch-hunting business, where you have no right to be.

"Private Stapp did nothing to affect national security. All

he did was exercise the rights you men swore to defend, the rights guaranteed by the United States Constitution.

"You have no choice, it seems to me, except to retain Private Stapp on the active-duty lists for the remainder of his eighty-two days. I also hope that the man—whoever he is—who decided that the United States Army's time should be wasted, that Private Stapp's time should be wasted and that the taxpayers' money should be wasted on this ridiculous proceeding, I hope that that man will be reprimanded and sent wherever reprimanded officers belong. Thank you."

The president of the board told us that we would be notified of their decision at "the proper time."

The Field Board Hearing was over. It would be more than two months before I learned its result.

But we all felt flushed with victory. The brass had worked hard to make the hearing an intimidating example to all dissenters. They had brought in a bird Colonel from Fourth Army Command to prosecute me and another full Colonel from the Defense Intelligence Agency of the Pentagon as a "security adviser." In spite of this awesome array of big brass, every GI witness, whether called by the Government or by the defense, stuck up for me and the union. It didn't really matter now what the board decided. We had turned the hearing around, the GIs felt stronger than ever, and we had gained time to keep on organizing.

Support for a GI union had begun to snowball. *The Bond* had been distributed at more than seventy-five bases, and letters were pouring into our New York headquarters by the hundreds. Many of the writers wanted to join immediately, others wanted more information, 99 percent supported the idea of the union. The letters came from Germany, France,

Vietnam, the Philippines, Okinawa, everywhere GIs are stationed. Fayette Richardson, who was holding down the fort in New York, couldn't handle the mounting work alone. Fayette had a job, a family to support, and even though he was devoting every spare moment to the union, there simply weren't enough hours in the day for him to put out *The Bond* and also accept memberships, to say nothing of answering the requests for information. Fayette enlisted another civilian, John Cat, who also had a family to take care of, but whose enthusiasm for the union was so great that he began devoting as much time as Richardson. Cat answered letters, an enormous task that his wife helped with, and still they couldn't keep up. Cat also found new ways to distribute *The Bond*. In fact, he initiated a tradition that endures to this day. He knew a lot of students who wanted to be active in the movement, including quite a few expecting induction, and with the students as a nucleus, he organized Sunday-evening distributions of *The Bond* at the Port Authority Bus Terminal in Manhattan. Fort Dix soldiers, returning to base after a weekend in the city, descended on the terminal by the thousands each Sunday. These GIs faced another week of hard work, inspections, belt-polishing, drilling, Army food and the brass. Soon they began looking forward to *The Bond*. It didn't pull any punches. It said what most GIs were thinking and what they would get court-martialed for if they said. Often the brass stationed MPs next to the students, and the MPs told passing soldiers that the paper was "subversive." Most GIs gave the MPs the bird. Few were intimidated.

More than anything else, these Sunday-evening distributions of *The Bond* account for the birth of our union chapter at Fort Dix.

The increasing activity at the national office of the American Servicemen's Union in New York City absorbed my attention more and more. The weeks I had remaining in the Army seemed almost unbearably long.

There were a few good reasons for still being at Fort Sill, however. One was Bob Lemay, the Vietnam veteran who had pushed his way past MPs to be at my Field Board Hearing despite his commanding officer's warning to stay away. Lemay had become friends with Dick Wheaton after returning from Vietnam. Their friendship became closer after Lemay's commanding officer told him to "stay away from those Communists, Wheaton and Stapp." Lemay said that nobody was going to tell him whom he was permitted to associate with. Likewise, nobody was going to keep him away from an "open" Field Board Hearing.

Bob Lemay talked a lot about Vietnam. He told of Quonset huts being used as hospitals for the Vietnamese, of how the only medicine was aspirin and Band-Aids, of people dying on bare bunks because there was no one to treat them. Lemay had seen and heard George Romney, campaigning for the Presidency, slap the backs of critically wounded GIs and say "Hiya, buddy," and "Good work," and "You should be proud of yourself."

The incident that made the most lasting impression on Lemay occurred when he took part in the search of a Vietnamese village. Without warning, his company descended on the village at dawn and drove the people out of their homes. Males were herded into one compound, females into another, and there they remained for the entire day while soldiers ransacked their homes. As was usually the case on these missions, nothing was found.

Lemay was discharged from the Army six months after I was. He and his wife Sherry came straight to New York and joined the staff of the American Servicemen's Union.

During my last two months at Fort Sill I encountered a

number of examples of how the brass can arbitrarily use their authority to make sure GIs toe the line. Rodney Oshiro was a Japanese-American, a corporal, and his lieutenant had been riding him for two months: "Hey, slant-eyes, who won World War II?"

Oshiro, realizing the lieutenant was simply prejudiced against Orientals, was nevertheless relieved when he himself was transferred to another part of the unit; he thought he had seen the last of his tormentor. Unfortunately, when Oshiro, preparing to leave, went to the orderly room to pick up his belongings, he found the lieutenant waiting for him.

"What the hell are you doing here, Oshiro?"

"I came to get my things."

"Get the hell out!"

"I'd be obliged to."

The lieutenant promptly initiated charges against Oshiro for not saying "sir" and for having a disrespectful inflection in his voice.

Dick Ilg was in Oshiro's unit. The two men had been friends for a year. Oshiro went to Ilg and told him about the charges. He said that his commanding officer had advised him to take an Article 15—an admission of guilt and the same thing as copping a plea. The inducement for doing this is that the punishment *might* be less than a court-martial, though there is no guarantee. Article 15 is simply a device the Army uses to spare itself the bother and publicity of a trial. Ilg assured Oshiro that the union would support him if he wanted his day in court. Oshiro simply didn't think he was guilty of anything. He told his commanding officer that if they were going to punish him they would first have to try him.

We engaged Rudolph Schware from Denver, the lawyer who had represented me at my second court-martial, to handle Oshiro's case. The NECLC had done a lot of rescue work for us without charging a cent; this time we decided to raise some money to at least partially reimburse them. We took up a collection in the barracks. Every single GI made a donation.

At the court-martial one of the Army's own witnesses testified that Oshiro was "as fine a soldier as anyone in the battalion." That didn't cut any ice; Oshiro had forgotten to "sir" an officer, and his "tone had been disrespectful."

The lieutenant took the stand and was asked to imitate the tone of disrespect. He cleared his throat and said, with a rising inflection, "I'd be obliged to," but it didn't sound very disrespectful. So he tried again, with a descending note in his voice: "I'd be obliged to." Titters broke out in the courtroom and the lieutenant's face reddened. On his third attempt he put his whole heart in the performance. "I'd be—" he began, but the judge broke in: "I think we understand. You're excused now."

Was Oshiro cleared? Hardly. He was reprimanded and reduced in rank from corporal to private, with a substantial cut in pay—$70 a month less than he had been getting.

The GIs in Oshiro's unit were boiling. He had been liked by everyone except the lieutenant. Many of the men came to me and said they wanted to join the union. They figured that if a man could lose $70 a month for forgetting to say "sir," they were all in jeopardy. When the lieutenant had told Oshiro to "get the hell out," that was all right with the Army. The lieutenant hadn't said "sir," and the tone of his voice had been anything but respectful, but he was an officer and a gentleman and above the laws of courtesy and respect.

Some organizers at other bases were more savagely attacked by the brass than we were at Fort Sill. In February 1968, at Fort Ord, California, Privates Ken Stolte and Dan Amick were court-martialed for passing out leaflets opposing the war and for supporting a union for service-men. Because of the leaflet the Army charged Stolte and Amick with "promoting disaffection among the troops." Stolte and Amick each received four years in prison.

Stolte wrote to *The Bond:* "You can't have a war with-out an Army. If only the GI would realize that he, more than anyone else, can do so much toward ending this sense-less slaughter. Perhaps some will go to jail, as I have, but it will be fruitful if it helps end the war."

As I mentioned, I was becoming increasingly eager to get out of the Army. There was little more I could do as a GI. But as a civilian and the head of a union that had strong backing from its members, well, that would be something else, something the hardened-in-amber brass had never fought before. I wanted to be out of the Army especially so I could help people like Ken Stolte and Dan Amick.

On April 19, 1968, less than four weeks before my tour of duty was up, the Field Board announced its decision: I was given an undesirable discharge. The board's findings were secret, so we never did learn why I was undesirable. We had a pretty good idea, though.

PART TWO

CHAPTER XIII   I was out of the Army, but the
fight against the Army had just begun. When I arrived in
New York City there were so many things to do it was difficult to know where to start. Deirdre and I rented an apartment and then found a small office on Fifth Avenue near
Twentieth Street and made it the headquarters of *The Bond*
and of the American Servicemen's Union.

The first thing the union needed was funds. If we were
going to continue to print a newspaper and send organizers
to Army bases to support soldiers facing the ire of the brass,
we would have to have money. And we didn't want to take
it from already strapped GIs. Fortunately a solution presented itself. Both Dick Wheaton, who had been discharged
a week before me, and I began to receive requests to speak
on college campuses. We were offered fees ranging from
$50 to $200, with all expenses paid. Naturally we jumped at
the opportunities. Not only could we make money for the
union but we could get our views across to large numbers of
young people, many of whom would soon be facing induction.

We had long since agreed that none of us would be paid
by the union, and that all the money we raised would go
into the union's account. We were too well aware of how an

ideal can be corrupted once somebody starts to profit from it. All of us had felt a sense of betrayal when the activism of people like Bob Dylan declined in direct relation to the growth of their bank accounts. Too often we had heard older people wave off the idealism of the young with, "Wait'll they start making money; then they won't be so interested in changing the system."

Of course, the need for enough money to pay for food and rent is not something you can just ignore. We solved this problem by taking part-time jobs at night. I found work in the mail room of a large retail firm.

We had another reason for not taking compensation from the union. The brass, typically, were openly threatening any GI who joined the union. We figured they were massing their thunderbolts to hurl at us in an effort to discredit the union in the eyes of prospective members. We certainly weren't going to let them say that we were enriching ourselves at the expense of enlisted men.

The brass began trying to infiltrate the union from the first day we set up headquarters on Fifth Avenue. They attempted to place informers in the union to learn what we were doing; unhappily for them, we were kept better informed of their actions than they were of ours.

For example, one of our members was an aide to the Commanding General of the United States Continental Army Command. She furnished us with some of the "secret" letters the General received. Since this GI is now out of the Army, I'll quote one of the letters—stamped "Confidential" four times—that she sent us. It was from Major G. A. Smith to the Commanding General.

CONFIDENTIAL

Subject: American Servicemen's Union—Introduction of Subversive Literature at Army Installations.

To: Commanding General, United States Continental Army Command

ATTN: ATINT-SCTY

Fort Monroe, Virginia 23351

1. By letter dated 4 May 1968, PVT. David W. ORT, allegedly representing the American Servicemen's Union, wrote a letter to the Commanding General, Fort Campbell, Kentucky, asking for official recognition. PVT. ORT's letter to the Commanding General contained five preliminary proposals for consideration (Enclosure 1—letter, American Servicemen's Union, National Office in New York, local representative, PVT. David W. ORT).

2. The Chief of Staff, Fort Campbell, replied to PVT. ORT that members of the Armed Services are prohibited from organizing or engaging in unionizing activities in connection with their military service. He stated further that the Command would not recognize or negotiate with such an organization or with PVT. ORT as their alleged representative (Enclosure 2— 1st Endorsement, dated 12 June 1968, subject: American Servicemen's Union).

3. Michael J. Kennedy, staff counsel, National Emergency Civil Liberties Committee, by letter requested authority and citation for the Chief of Staff's statements (Enclosure 3). Upon the advice of the Staff Judge Advocate, Fort Campbell, Kennedy's letter has not been answered.

4. Additional efforts may be made to establish the American Servicemen's Union at other installations. Guidance is needed as to the proper manner of dealing with such requests and/or proposals.

5. A second problem concerns AR 381-135, "Control of Subversive Publications Disseminated at Army Installations," which contained basic policy, defined responsibilities and outlined authority of the installation commander to control dissemination of commercial publications considered to be subversive or otherwise detrimental to the loyalty or morale of the troops. The regulation has been rescinded and no other regulation is currently in force which deals with the subject in the same way. Servicemen in the Army under the jurisdiction of this headquarters known to have subversive or dissident

tendencies are disseminating dissident/subversive-type literature within the installations at which they are stationed. To date, there is no definite policy under which installation commanders can control the dissemination of such material. Many of these publications, in fact, will cite the statement that the publication is the personal property of the individual who has it and that it may not be taken from him. Instances of individual soldiers having several hundred copies of such publications as *The Daily Worker, The Vietnam GI, Ally, Challenge, Act,* and other similar pieces, pose a positive threat to the loyalty and morale of the troops. With an indication of an expansion of this activity within Third US Army area, it is considered advisable that a determination be made defining the installation commander's authority for control of such subversive material by confiscation or other means.

6. It is requested that guidance be furnished so that installations may have a definite policy with which to operate in their areas.

G. A. SMITH
MAJ, AGC
ASST AG

So much for G. A. Smith.

Richardson, Wheaton, Cat and I began mailing out union membership cards to GIs who had told us they wanted to join. One dollar was charged for a one-year membership. By the middle of May 1968 we had more than one thousand members, representing some seventy-five bases both here and abroad.

It was only the beginning, because these one thousand GIs were all eager to enlist new members. And we were getting plenty of publicity too. *Esquire* magazine ran a cover story titled "The Plot to Unionize the U.S. Army."

A full-page story in *Time* was captioned "Bugging the Brass."

The New York *Post* did an editorial that ended with a warning to the brass: "Remember Republic Steel."

The main reason GIs turn to the ASU is the brass. If there is a wrong way to react, the brass can be counted on to find it. When the *Esquire* story hit the stands (the picture on the cover showed a private sticking his tongue out at a General) the brass banned it from many Army bases, which, of course, was the best way to assure that GIs would seek out a copy.

From the outset the American Servicemen's Union was kept busy answering requests for help. Typical of these was the case of Fred Patrick. Patrick, a naval airman apprentice, walked into our office on June 6, 1968, and told us that he had been AWOL from El Centro Naval Air Station in California for more than three months. Patrick's job had been to fuel Navy fighter planes, and he had heard pilots talk about the destruction of entire villages by saturation bombing in the *hope* that NLF people were quartered there. Patrick hitchhiked to New York and stayed in hiding until he heard about the ASU.

I asked Patrick what he wanted to do. Did he want to leave the country? He said that he didn't, that he wanted to turn himself in if he could count on civilian help. We told him that was one of the reasons we were in business.

Members of the ASU and the Committee for GI Rights accompanied Patrick to the Brooklyn Naval Base, where he turned himself in, which he did by throwing his uniform at the feet of the officer of the day.

"Pick it up."

"No."

"Pick it up!"

"I'm going to tell you why I cannot serve in the Armed Forces of this country. I will not be brought before a war-crimes tribunal now or in the future and be charged with the killing and maiming of helpless civilians and the wanton destruction of homes and crops."

Patrick was imprisoned in the Brooklyn brig pending his trial. While in jail he signed thirty new members into the union—including five guards!

Once again the tireless Michael Kennedy of NECLC came to the rescue. Members of CGIR (Committee for GI Rights) and YAWF joined the ASU people at the trial. We knew the more people we could gather to protest, the more news coverage Fred would get, and, most important, the more civilians would become aware of the brutal injustices perpetrated by courts-martial boards.

The Navy could have charged Fred Patrick with desertion, since any man AWOL more than thirty days is technically a deserter, but instead they charged him with the lesser offense of being AWOL. This wasn't because Patrick's plight had touched the hearts of the Navy brass. There just aren't enough jails, stockades and brigs to hold the tens of thousands of GIs who go AWOL each year for more than thirty days. One ASU member was AWOL for twenty-three months, and the Army was so happy to get him back that his only punishment was a fine of one month's pay.

With the help of YAWF and CGIR we threw a picket line around the disciplinary restriction barracks where Patrick's trial was to be held.

Michael Kennedy and I were detained when we tried to enter the courtroom.

"Who are you birds?" the guard asked.

"I'm the attorney for the accused," Kennedy said. "Let us by."

But just then the assorted marines, secret police and Federal marshals keeping an eye on the picket line and the entrance to the courthouse were thrown into confusion. A large white sheet had descended from a window in the restricted section of the barracks. Written on the sheet in bold black letters was: "We Support the American Servicemen's Union."

The sheet was the work of Patrick's fellow prisoners. It fluttered for ten minutes before the guards were able to tear it down. By that time Kennedy and I had slipped into the courtroom.

On the court-martial board were a captain, two lieutenant commanders and three ensigns. Kennedy began by asking the lieutenant commanders whether they would obey an order that violated the United States Constitution.

Both said they would, and Kennedy succeeded in getting them disqualified. Then he dismissed the captain, who had been serving as president of the court, with the one peremptory challenge allowed the defense. The trial continued with only the three ensigns on the board.

Then Kennedy began the argument that would make headlines the next day in *The New York Times*. It went like this: "Conscientious objectors are exempt from combat duty. They are exempt by law. Fred Patrick is a conscientious objector. Therefore, when he is ordered to Vietnam he has the right to obey the law and disobey the illegal order. He has the right to go AWOL."

Kennedy, speaking softly, asked the judge if this wasn't so.

The judge said it was.

The headline in *The New York Times* read: "Conscientious Objection Gives Right to Go AWOL."

Of course, such was hardly the case. After a "what-in-the-world-are-you-doing?" call from an Admiral at the Pentagon, the judge overruled himself and ordered the trial to continue.

But Kennedy's bag of tricks was inexhaustible. With an innocent voice that masked the cunning of a fox, he said he wanted to raise a legal point covered in the *BUPERS Manual*. The *BUPERS Manual* is a military law text, and it is illegal for officers sitting on court-martial boards to consult it during a trial.

Kennedy asked the three ensigns: "Have you gentlemen ever read the *BUPERS Manual?*"

The three said they had.

"Good," Kennedy said. "The point I want to raise is covered there. I hope the book's contents are fresh in your minds."

The lieutenant commanders would never have fallen for it. But these were ensigns, eager to prove their expertise, and they assured Kennedy that they were most familiar with the *BUPERS Manual.* One even volunteered that he had been reading it the night before.

Kennedy turned to the judge and asked for a mistrial, and there was nothing the man could do but grant it.

Fred Patrick was brought to trial a second time, and on this occasion the brass won, but the case received the kind of headlines they don't like. Outside the courtroom were hundreds of antiwar demonstrators and inside were five naval enlisted men in their whites who sat through the entire trial in Patrick's support.

Fred Patrick was sentenced to six months in prison. The brass feared he might recruit other inmates, so they kept him in solitary confinement the entire time.

By July 1968 the American Servicemen's Union had grown to more than two thousand members. Not only had soldiers joined but sailors, marines and airmen. We even had several WACS and WAVES, and our members were on almost every base in the world. Most important, virtually every union member was an organizer.

We also began to be swamped by requests for help. Enlisted men facing courts-martial knew better than to trust their defense to officers. When we could we obtained free aid from NECLC, ACLU, the Workers Defense League and the National Lawyers Guild. When we couldn't we paid civilian lawyers out of union funds. A serviceman does not have to be a member of ASU to receive help. Many GIs wanted to join but were afraid to. At Fort Lewis, where union membership had mushroomed, Colonel G. V. Reberry thought he could put the skids under our union by posting the following warning: "No member of this command will disseminate, distribute or post material or publications whose subject matter promotes disloyalty or discontent, nor will they attempt to gain the sympathy of persons for membership in organizations which advocate dissension or disaffiliation."

That's what Colonel Reberry thinks. But the truth is, the Fort Lewis chapter of the American Servicemen's Union has more than doubled since he posted his edict.

Sp/4 Niel Chaker, an ASU organizer at Fort Lewis, put his reply to Reberry's warning right next to it on the unit bulletin board. Chaker wrote:

> Let's tell it like it is, Colonel. We are not discontented by what we read and hear. We are discontented because of the way we live. Discontent is not caused by newspapers but by harassment and lack of freedom.
>
> We could take the low pay, lousy food and rotten living conditions if we thought that what we were doing was worthwhile or beneficial to the country. But we don't think so.
>
> Our dissension will end when the conditions that cause it end. You may succeed in driving dissension underground but you can never stop it. You may be able to extract sullen obedience as long as MPs are in range, but you will never get loyalty.
>
> We are citizens, covered by the Bill of Rights. Your warning violates the Bill of Rights.

But most encouraging were the letters. They came by the hundreds, from places like Fort Polk (Louisiana), West Germany, Ethiopia, Panama, Spain, Italy, Turkey and South Korea (the United States has troops in all those places, in 109 foreign countries in all).

It was from the letters we received from Vietnam, however, that we learned how desperately GIs need a union to champion their cause. One letter in particular, smuggled from the Long Binh Jail (appropriately called the LBJ), revealed what happens to enlisted men who try to fight the brass alone. After relating the unfit-for-a-pig conditions at LBJ, the letter described some of the "crimes" that had landed the men in prison. One infantryman had received a six-month sentence for stealing a peanut butter sandwich from the base mess hall. Another had been sentenced to a year for refusing to obey an order: the order was to beat a confession out of an NLF prisoner. A third received four months for "forgetting" to salute an officer. A fourth, a black GI, was sentenced to three *years* for "assaulting" a white soldier who flew the Confederate flag from his pup tent.

But these were nothing compared to what happened to the GI who, with less than two months to serve in Vietnam, was sent along with seventeen other men to attack a force of two hundred and fifty North Vietnamese. This GI was the only survivor, and he was wounded in the right arm, the right leg and the kidneys. He was sent to Japan to recuperate, and while he was there the Army lost his medical records. He was denied further treatment and returned to Vietnam. When he refused to go back into combat, the brass court-martialed him, and he had been awaiting trial for two months when we received his letter. A civilian could obtain bond and be free while awaiting trial, but there is no such thing as bail in the Army.

Stockade prisoners at Long Binh don't salute in the usual way. They are forced to take off their caps and slap them against their legs. Besides the filthy and meager food ration, the crowding at Long Binh was intolerable. Seven hundred and nineteen prisoners were packed into quarters designed for two hundred and fifty. We knew from the tone of the letters smuggled to us that tensions were building up to an explosion.

It came on August 29, 1968. Just before midnight, in a barbed-wire-enclosed "medium security" section, guards heard shouting and the sounds of a scuffle. Three guards, thinking a fight had broken out, rushed in and were immediately taken captive. The prisoners seized their keys and broke out into the main compound. They burned nine buildings to the ground, one of which contained their records. The brass, commanded by Colonel William Brandenburg of Elloree, South Carolina, sent in MPs with rifles, bayonets and gas grenades. The unarmed prisoners fought back. They injured five MPs and put the acting warden in the hospital. But it was a costly demonstration. One GI was killed and fifty-nine were wounded. News reports as late as September 24, 1968, told of twelve black GIs still bravely holding out in an isolated section of the prison.

Thirteen days before the Long Binh revolt a similar uprising took place in the marine brig at Danang. The grievances were comparable, though there was one that had not been on the list of the Long Binh prisoners: at Danang, guards had to be saluted. It took a force of 75 shotgun-firing MPs to crush the 288 unarmed prisoners who revolted at Danang. And it still wasn't over. Two days later a second rebellion broke out.

As chairman of the American Servicemen's Union (seventeen ASU members were involved in the Danang revolts), I telephoned the Pentagon and demanded to know what was being done to the prisoners. We had heard that some of them were being beaten and that others were close to starvation, because, as one captain allegedly said, "We've got to teach them a lesson."

Lieutenant Colonel Ludvig, Director of Marine Public Relations, refused to issue any information, "not to you, the press or anybody."

CHAPTER XIV   On April 4, 1968, Martin Luther King, Jr., was shot in Memphis, and his assassination touched off rebellions in 110 cities. Carrying out the Pentagon's long-prepared "Operation Garden Plot," 15,000 Army troops were called to assist 45,000 National Guardsmen and countless city policemen. Two thousand soldiers were flown from Fort Sill to Baltimore to put down a revolt. More important to this story, 5,000 GIs from Fort Hood, many of them black men, were rushed to Chicago to rescue Daley City. When they arrived they learned that the mayor had ordered looters and arsonists shot on sight. Now, this was just a little too much for black GIs to stomach. When they returned to Fort Hood they vowed they would never go to Chicago again.

Then came August and an uprising in a Miami ghetto during the Republican National Convention. Four black youths died in that uprising while rich delegates were wheeling and dealing in the fetid atmosphere of smoke-filled back rooms.

Late in August came Chicago and the Democratic National Circus. The stupidity of the brass, their thick-skinned callousness, their utter disregard for the most basic human feelings, all were glaringly evident when they ordered black

GIs at Fort Hood to return to Chicago to help maintain Mayor Daley's security. It was as though the British had sent Irish troops to quell the Easter Rebellion. These black GIs thought they were being sent to Chicago to put down fellow blacks and they wanted to have nothing to do with it.

Indeed, it was fear of an uprising in Chicago's black community that prompted the brass to send the troops. But this action even went against the Army's own policy. The Army always sends soldiers from a distant state to put down a riot in another state. They want to arouse as little sympathy as possible. They do not want friends or brothers facing each other over the barrel of a gun. But what the brass did not understand, could not possibly understand, is that all black people are neighbors, friends and brothers, no matter what corner of the land they are born in.

Among the Fort Hood soldiers ordered to Chicago were the same black GIs who had been sickened by Mayor Daley's shoot-to-kill order in April and who had vowed they would never fight against their brothers again for any cause, especially Richard Daley's. On August 23, at 9 P.M., more than one hundred of these black GIs massed for a protest demonstration.

At midnight the Commandant of the First Armored Division, General Boles, came to plead (not order—plead) with the men to disperse. Boles gave an impassioned speech, in the course of which he proved his absence of racial prejudice: "I don't have anything against Negroes. I have a Negro boy working at my house."

The black GIs were unmoved. And fearing that there might possibly be massive support from white GIs for these black protesters, Boles became even more conciliatory. He raised his right hand and said the men could stay where they were all night without repercussions. Eight other brass hats

—all Colonels—witnessed this concession. However, when some of the black GIs asked Boles to sign a statement concerning what he had just said, he refused and left the area.

The men stayed all night. At dawn MPs came and arrested forty-three of them for failure to report for reveille.

Twenty-five of the forty-three were veterans of the Vietnam war. Eight had been decorated for bravery.

In the stockade the forty-three men refused to obey orders until they were given legal aid. They even refused to eat. After eight hours of having his orders ignored, the commandant of the prison took off his steel helmet and swung it into the face of one of the prisoners. Then sixty MPs descended on the men with nightsticks. Fifty-eight of the MPs proceeded to administer brutal beatings; two of them were black and refused to take part in the assault.

The idea of helmeted guards swinging truncheons down on the heads of defenseless men is not a pleasant one. Is this perhaps an isolated instance of sadism? Unfortunately it is not. Resistance in the ranks is a phenomenon that dries the throats of the brass, that makes their hearts pound in dismay. The rules require that there be men to obey and others to command. Without this logic the game of warfare will not work. So the brass strive mightily to instill in the common soldier the thought of obedience, at all times, without question. The brass know they sit astride a sleeping giant, and their great fear is of the moment he may awake. When the soldier rouses himself from his compliant stupor and begins to question his predicament, then the brass are in trouble, and they know it. Their only answers are force and blood and making examples of the few so as to terrify the many. They are literally fighting for their lives when they send clubs down on the heads of rebellious soldiers.

Some of the black GIs at Fort Hood had their skulls laid

open to the bone, but medical care was withheld for twenty-four hours.

Four hours after the men were arrested an American Servicemen's Union member called me at the ASU office and told me the story. I said the union would do all it could and phoned Michael Kennedy to ask for legal aid. Kennedy agreed to help but said he couldn't do anything until he knew the names of the defendants. I got in touch with both Fort Hood and the Pentagon, but was refused any information. Then I called the ASU member who had told me about the case and asked him if there was some way he could get the names. He said that his unit was being sent on maneuvers and he wouldn't have time. "But," he added, "my wife's able to help. She knows a black MP, and I think if he understands the reason we want the names, he'll cooperate."

The MP did cooperate, and within twenty-four hours we had all forty-three names along with their ranks and serial numbers.

Michael Kennedy immediately went to work, and Dick Wheaton, Bill Smith, John Cat and I began making plans to go to Fort Hood. This was the union's first chance to intervene in a case with multiple defendants, and we welcomed the opportunity to confront the brass.

No commercial flights stop in Killeen, Texas, which is the nearest town to Fort Hood, so we landed in Dallas and took an eight-passenger Cessna the rest of the way.

The moment we arrived in Killeen the heat closed in. It was more than 100 degrees, muggy, a gray-yellow morning that ate away the eyes and the spirit. Then an odor assailed us, pungent and powerful, nauseating, and our stomachs convulsed and turned over and the only way we could hold back the vomit was to clamp our jaws shut and stop breathing. Millions of dead locusts were everywhere, on sidewalks and gutters and rooftops, and they were decomposing under a fierce Texas sun. The stench of Killeen in August when the locusts die is a stink right out of the bowels of hell, something a man has to smell to believe; and he has to see the crude, cruel men who live in Killeen to believe them.

Until a few years ago a sign at the town's entrance bore the warning: "Niggers, don't let the sun set on your ass in Killeen." A Supreme Court decision and the Army's announced policy of desegregation combined to pressure the city fathers into taking it down, but it still hangs there in the minds of thousands of black GIs at Fort Hood.

The young men of Killeen, sons of local merchants for the most part, have banded into a club whose sole purpose is to beat up GIs. The club was formed after these young people found it difficult to get dates. For reasons obvious to anyone who has ever visited Killeen, the girls in the town prefer GIs, a fact not likely to promote harmony between the local bucks and the soldiers. So the locals formed a gang they call "The Goat Ropers." To distinguish themselves from GIs, the Goat Ropers wear their own uniform: ten-gallon hats, boots, spurs, lassos, bandanas and cartridge belts.

The only person a Goat Roper hates more than a white GI is a black GI. The day before we arrived the Goat Ropers beat up a black GI and left him unconscious in an alley. The black GI came to in a local jail charged with assault.

But the charge of vagrancy is the favorite device of the Killeen police. It is used against anyone the police consider undesirable. Seventeen-year-old Jesse Delgado was a Mexican-American living with his parents in Killeen. Delgado was a civilian employee at Fort Hood and had become friendly with a number of antiwar, pro-union GIs. This, of course, made him undesirable, and the police arrested him for vagrancy and held him so long that he lost his job on the base. Then several days later, as he was mounting the courthouse steps to attend his trial on the first vagrancy charge, he was arrested again. The police weren't sure they could make the first charge stick, but they were certain of the second one; after all, Delgado had no job.

The face we saw most often in the streets of Killeen was that of George Wallace, the "champion of the little man." Wallace election posters were in bars, restaurants, bus stations; many cars bore his bumper stickers, in the windows of homes hung his picture.

The most popular meeting place for GIs in Killeen is the Oleo Strut, which has recently received national attention in newspapers and magazines. The citizens of Killeen, led by the Reverend Bob Johnson, have been trying to close down the Oleo Strut because "It's a meeting place for undesirables." Time and again the police have raided this GI hangout, on the grounds, I suppose, that they might find Communists, though I believe any self-respecting red could easily deceive their keen, perceptive eyes.

In a letter to a national magazine, one enlisted man (not an ASU member) of Washington, D.C., said: "I was stationed in Killeen, Texas, for seven months, and I'd like to know how often—if ever—the Reverend Bob Johnson has actually been to the Oleo Strut. I went to the Oleo Strut and I wear the Silver Star with a 'V' for valor, as well as two Purple Hearts. I was wounded in the arms and chest in Vietnam. Reverend Johnson, if I'm undesirable *you* go fight in Vietnam instead of me."

Dan Scott, now stationed at Fort Leonard Wood, Missouri, went to a church in Killeen and was thrown out because his hair was too long. He went to another church and the preacher began his sermon by saying: "There are good niggers. They know their place. But there are bad niggers, too, those who don't know their place. Those are the ones we have to guard against."

Loan sharks flourish in Killeen, winked at by the police. They charge 30 percent a week and have goon squads to beat up late-paying GIs.

After we rented a hotel room John Cat and I set out for the Judge Advocate General's office at Fort Hood. I had a letter signed by Michael Kennedy saying that I was his agent and asking that I be allowed to talk with the prisoners. The night before, the brass had posted a warning telling all personnel "to be on the lookout for Andrew D. Stapp." The bulletin told GIs not to associate with me, that I was a "subversive," and gave an accurate description of my height and weight. It was not difficult to figure out who had told the brass I was coming. Two of J. Edgar Hoover's sleuths had for weeks been standing outside the American Servicemen's Union office looking clumsy and trying to get the names of everyone who visited us. The FBI also had our phone bugged and was following me, though only J. Edgar knows why.

A generation of Americans have now grown up under the shadow of this man. To many people it is a comforting shadow, an umbrella, as it were, symbolizing the incorruptible true-blue father figure protecting his children, warning them away from evil paths, directing them in the tread of those pioneers who made this country what it is. They are welcome to that image. There are others who feel less comforted, who wonder how one man is able, for forty years and more, to survive every transfer of power, every shift of policy, and still maintain his grip on the pinnacle, inscrutable, answerable to no one, capable of preventing the least glimmer of publicity from entering his life, and above all, enforcing his will, by wiretap, by innuendo, by the subtle yet complete destruction of those who dare to oppose him. He calls others dangerous, yet he is one of the most dangerous men in the world.

Although the warning the brass had posted at Fort Hood accurately described my weight and height, it erroneously stated that I had a beard. I had never had a beard, or even long hair, and I am certain the FBI didn't say I had. It was the brass, and their mistake is understandable. To them all subversives have beards.

At the Judge Advocate General's office I handed Kennedy's letter to a Captain Henig. He must have thought I was a lawyer because he didn't even question my request to see the prisoners. He told Cat and me that the black GIs had been temporarily released and were under barracks arrest because "There isn't enough room in the stockade." He added, however, that a group was due for release and that he expected to fill the vacancies immediately.

We thanked Henig and headed for the barracks. I think it was the only time I have ever been happy to be on an Army base. The stink of the rotting locusts didn't reach as far as Fort Hood.

We talked with a number of the black GIs in the barracks and they said they were glad we had come. Among them was Alvin Henry, who had earned the Silver Star for "risking his life to carry a wounded sergeant to a medical evacuation helicopter"; Walter Waites, who had served eighteen months in Vietnam even though he had lost a brother there; and Bob Rucker, who had received a Leadership Plaque, an Army Commendation and a Bronze Star.

Cat and I told them about Michael Kennedy and the NECLC and how well they had handled GI cases before. Even though a few of the black GIs were union members, they were at first hesitant to trust us. Bitter experience had

taught them to question the motives of white men. But in the
end they accepted our help, thanks mainly to Bob Rucker,
whom they had appointed their spokesman. After a while
Rucker said, "These guys are okay," and that was that.

Bob Rucker had had only three more weeks to serve in
the Army when he had risked a five-year prison sentence to
participate in the Fort Hood demonstration. He could have
stayed in his bunk that night and not one of his friends
would have blamed him. It was no wonder they respected
him. Yet this winner of the Bronze Star would be accused of
cowardice at his court-martial because he had refused to go
to Chicago.

During my stint in the Army I had heard plenty of Vietnam horror stories, but talking to the black GIs in the Fort
Hood barracks I was destined to learn more. One of them
told of the time he had been assigned a job usually handled
by a dog. His commanding officer hadn't known whether an
area was mined, so the black GI was sent ahead to find out.
Had he been blown up, the officer would have instructed the
others not to proceed. This same black GI, while walking
down a muddy trail near Danang with a pack on his shoulder, was stopped by a sergeant and asked, "Why not carry
that on your head the way the niggers in Africa do?"

Ernest Frederick was one black GI we didn't get to see in
the barracks. It seems the stockade hadn't been *that*
crowded, so Frederick was kept behind barbed wire. Incidentally, Frederick's discharge papers were three days away
from being signed when he took part in the protest.

Cat and I went to Frederick's commanding officer and
asked permission to visit the stockade. The commanding
officer was very cooperative. He even loaned us his jeep.
But our luck was soon to run out.

The stockade sergeant read Kennedy's letter four times.

He kept looking at me, then at the letter, then up in the sky. My name rang a bell. Finally he remembered the bulletin. But where was the beard? I must have shaved it, he decided, and headed for the stockade commandant's office with a "Wait here" tossed back over his shoulder.

Ten minutes later we were in the comfortable office of Major Openlander, the stockade commandant. Openlander's voice sounded as though he regularly swallowed the barbed wire his guards so liberally deployed. "So you want to see Frederick," he said. "You'll have to go to the Provost Marshal to get a pass."

Openlander drove us to the Provost Marshal's office and deposited us in an empty room. The first person to show up was a lieutenant colonel. He took a seat at the opposite end of the room, gave us a look of distaste and said nothing. Then came another lieutenant colonel. Then two full bird Colonels. Finally an MP. He was the first to break the metallic silence. "Let me have your letter," he said, and I handed it to him thinking he was going to show it to the brass hats. Instead the MP walked out of the room and Cat and I continued to smile at the unsmiling officers.

Finally the Provost Marshal, Colonel Gaereke, appeared. Gaereke had snow-white hair and apple-colored cheeks. "Stapp," he said, "you've been barred from every military reservation in the country."

"That's not true and I want my letter back."

"You're not getting your letter back. You're not even leaving. We're holding you here."

"I'm not a private in your goddam Army any more. You can't tell me what to do."

"Can't I?" Gaereke turned and walked out the door.

Cat and I got up and walked past the solemn-faced brass hats still in the room. The MP who had taken my letter, and who was now guarding the door, looked at one of the full bird Colonels but got a blank stare in return, so he didn't try to stop us.

We had walked all the way out to Fort Hood and we started to walk back. We had accomplished most of what we had hoped to. The black GIs had accepted our offer of help. They had been in favor of our plan to bring a supporting delegation to their courts-martial. They had even been enthusiastic about the petition we intended to circulate at every base where the ASU had members, though they had pointed out, and we had had to agree, that the brass are not much impressed by petitions or demonstrations. I was reminded of the Pentagon General who, after 250,000 people had marched on his building in 1967, remarked that "There are two hundred million citizens in this country; considering that figure, a quarter-million is a pretty small minority."

Cat and I had not gone three hundred yards before Gaereke puffed up behind us. He was accompanied by Openlander and an FBI agent who started to photograph us with his camera.

"Let's get out of the sun and talk this over," Gaereke said.

"No, thanks," I said.

Gaereke then produced a sheet of paper that he tried to hand to me. I let it flutter to the ground. It was a bar order forbidding me to set foot on Fort Hood property.

We survived in Killeen for four more days. We weren't allowed to talk with the court-martialed GIs, but we had plenty to keep us busy. We mailed petitions protesting the courts-martial by special delivery letters to union members at bases all over the world. We collected signatures from five hundred Fort Hood GIs. We sent out press releases to the news media to alert them about what was happening.

Some unexpected and welcome visitors arrived in Killeen

—a carload of Committee for GI Rights people from New York. These civilians had jobs and families to take care of, yet they were involved enough to come to this dreary Texas cow town to demonstrate their support for their black brothers and against the brass.

Michael Kennedy came to Killeen for a pretrial hearing and we had dinner together. "Andy," he said, "you'd better leave town. They're out to get you."

It was the kind of warning a lawyer feels he has to give. Kennedy knew damn well I wasn't leaving, and neither were the other ASU and CGIR people.

Unfortunately Kennedy knew what he was talking about. The next morning the police arrested Bill Smith, Dick Wheaton and me. The charge: vagrancy. The police took our shoelaces, belts, ties and socks so we wouldn't hang ourselves and locked us in separate cells. I thought we might be there for the duration, but Kennedy kicked up such a fuss that three hours later we were brought before Judge John Odom. Judge John Odom was the former mayor of Killeen and he had civic pride. Vagrants were not to be tolerated in his town.

"You have the right to remain silent," Judge Odom said. "Anything you say may be held against you."

"You've got to be kidding," Bill Smith said. "This isn't real."

"I assure you, young man, it's very real."

Then Smith made a mistake. "How can we be vagrants?" he asked. "We're legally registered in a Killeen motel. We have six hundred dollars altogether."

We were found guilty. The fine: six hundred dollars.

Thousands of signatures were collected by ASU members in support of the court-martialed Fort Hood GIs. Many Fort Hood enlisted men, despite warnings from the brass to stay away, came to the courts-martial. They were joined by servicemen who had demonstrated at Bergstrom Air Force Base the week before and by civilians from hundreds of miles around.

Correspondents from AP, UPI, *The New York Times* and *Time* magazine covered the trials. The publicity and pressure applied to the brass resulted in relatively light sentences—light, that is, compared to what other GIs had received for similar offenses—though the crime was that they were sentenced at all.

The final score was twenty-six convicted, thirteen acquitted and four who never went to trial.

The longest sentence was ten months at hard labor. The most common sentence was three months. Only a couple of the Vietnam war heroes were convicted. Although all of them had admitted being leaders of the demonstration, the brass didn't have the guts to find the rest guilty.

CHAPTER XV   Membership in the American Servicemen's Union reached twenty-five hundred in October 1968. Although we felt that was an impressive number for a union less than five months old, we knew our true strength was much more impressive. The thousands of signatures we had collected in support of the Fort Hood GIs proved that. But a lot of enlisted men, sympathetic to our cause, were afraid to join because they feared reprisals from the brass. And some of the things the brass were doing in October 1968 showed their threats against dissident GIs were not hollow. Nor had they become any more sensitive to basic human justice. Let me demonstrate what I mean.

Bruce Peterson, editor of Fort Hood's antiwar *Fatigue Press,* was sentenced to eight years in the stockade after police allegedly found three seeds of marijuana in his pocket. Part of an Army drive against drugs? Not likely. Shortly after Peterson's sentencing, Sp/4 John Steinbeck, son of the author and a Vietnam veteran, testified before a U.S. Senate subcommittee investigating drug abuse: "Our Government is drugging our soldiers to be better fighters." He told how amphetamines (speed) were dispensed by medical corpsmen to GIs in Vietnam. "The drug is very popular, especially to the combat soldier, because it gives him a superhuman amount of energy and in this way it can be said that it is beneficial to him as a fighting machine," Steinbeck said. Unlike the relatively harmless marijuana, amphetamines are considered by many doctors to be in a class with heroin.

Clarence Mills, a twenty-year-old Yakima-Cherokee Indian who was wounded in action in Vietnam, was arrested in Olympia, Washington, as he was entering the Thurston County courthouse to attend the trial of seven other Indians who had been jailed for demanding fishing rights. The charge against Mills? Saying, in conversations with friends, that he wouldn't go back to Vietnam.

Eight black GIs were arrested at Fort Jackson, South Carolina, for "listening to taped speeches of Malcolm X."

Navy Nurse Susan Schnall was court-martialed for "conduct unbecoming an officer" and for "impairing the morale, loyalty and discipline of the members of the Armed Forces." What Nurse Schnall had done was rent a plane and drop antiwar leaflets over Navy stations in the San Francisco area. She was sentenced to six months at hard labor and given a dishonorable discharge.

American Civil Liberties Union attorneys investigated reports that GIs were being tortured in the Fort Dix, New Jersey, stockade. The prisoners finally revolted when they were denied water with dinner. The Dix stockade, condemned as unfit by the Army over twenty years before, held three times the maximum number of inmates it was built for. After the uprising had been crushed the brass charged thirty-eight men with riot, inciting to riot, conspiracy to riot, aggravated arson and destruction of Government property. Four ASU members face charges that could bring them over forty-five years in prison.

One of these four is Terry Klug, the archetype of a union organizer. Given orders at Fort Bragg, North Carolina, to report for duty in Vietnam, Terry split for Italy. May 1968 found him in Paris fighting on the barricades in what almost became the first workers' revolution in Western Europe. Klug worked with the American deserters who drifted through France and helped put out a GI newspaper for the men stationed in Germany.

But it wasn't enough, Terry felt, merely to agitate among the GIs from the safety of his French sanctuary. He was convinced that he must return to the Armed Forces himself in order to carry on the fight more effectively. He did return and was sentenced to three years' hard labor.

In the few months between his desertion trial and the stockade rebellion at Fort Dix, Klug organized a powerful chapter of the ASU among the prisoners. Many of the inmates who became active with the ASU under Terry's leadership eventually became top-notch union organizers in their own right.

Terry Klug had originally been trained for work in Military Intelligence. A Department of the Army handbook describes M.I. in the following words:

"From the foggy streets of London to the teeming byways of Asian cities to the sidewalks of New York and San Francisco, Military Intelligence agents are hard at work. A career in this corps of special investigators is a career in police work with the Free World as a beat."

Klug wasn't impressed.

And the war went on. It went on because great numbers of Americans bemoaned their helplessness to stop the carnage while accepting the system that ordered it; because parents wrung their hands and yet dutifully surrendered their sons to die; because the arrogance of military commanders was condoned, even when it cost the lives of their men. The system surrounds the whole business of warfare with sonorous references to patriotism, defense of home and country and saving others from the "tentacles of Communism." It makes sure that the home folks are properly whipped up to pay at least lip service to the nobility of the common soldier. It invents lovely phrases like "Gold Star Mother" to make a bereft parent feel important and appreciated and to distract her from the reality of what has happened to her son.

But when, in spite of all their plans, someone rises to protest, the brass show their true spirit. They are like the emperor with his new clothes, watching for the small boy at the edge of the crowd. That is why they must hunt down the dissenters and make examples of them. Who knows, someday some enlisted man may get an idea and turn to his buddies and say, "Listen! There are more of us than there are of them!"

Faced with a rising tide of dissidence, General Stone issued his infamous salute-or-die order: "Any GI showing disrespect to an officer will be sent to the front."

This was a real landmark in keeping the men in line. I felt General Stone deserved my congratulations. I called the Pentagon and was diverted to the public relations officer.

"What the hell are you going to do about this order?"

"Not a thing," was the reply.

"What's your opinion of it?"

"I don't have an opinion."

"Well, we do. Either it's rescinded immediately or you'll see some real hell raised."

"Think you can fight the Government? Go ahead and try."

We contacted every newspaper and every radio and television station in New York City. We made plans for demonstrations at every Army base where the ASU has members. We decided on a massive campaign to alert the people about

General Stone. The Pentagon got wind of our plans and re-scinded Stone's order.

No one doubts the existence of a class system in the Army. At the top of the heap are the Generals, at the bottom the enlisted men. But not everyone realizes that the system extends to wives. On the rare occasions when GIs are invited to social functions attended by NCOs and officers, the invitations read: "Officers and their ladies, sergeants and their wives, enlisted men and their women."

Roger Priest, an ASU member, defied this military caste system and now faces thirty-nine years in the stockade. He is represented by David Rein, who defended me at my first court-martial.

The charges against Robert Priest are nothing short of preposterous, prominent among them being that of "showing disrespect to L. Mendel Rivers." Yes, L. Mendel Rivers, the same L. Mendel Rivers who praised Robert Welch, founder of the John Birch Society as "courageous and perceptive," the same L. Mendel Rivers who called Franco and his fascist army "the greatest allies we have, one of the few on earth I trust," the same L. Mendel Rivers who said "Flatten Hanoi and let world opinion go fly a kite."

Roger Priest was a Navy man assigned to a clerk's job at the Pentagon. A six-foot, five-inch, two-hundred-and-forty-pound Texas athlete with a thatch of blond hair, Priest was firmly opposed to the war. He began putting out a newspaper, again supported by the ASU. One of the articles he published was a satiric fable that portrayed L. Mendel Rivers as a barnyard animal that was polluting a once-clear stream. This fable wounded the sensibilities of the congressman from South Carolina, and L. Mendel Rivers, as chairman of the House Armed Services Committee, is not a man the brass like to see offended. But a court-martial? For disrespect? To L. Mendel Rivers?

Some of the other charges against Priest—all of them stemming from articles that appeared in his newspaper—include:

"Showing disrespect for General Earle Wheeler."

This charge arose from the article first printed in *The Bond,* and reprinted both in Priest's newspaper and, in part, in this book, that contrasted my beliefs with Wheeler's.

"Advocating overthrow of the Government."

Priest wrote in his newspaper that "we will do anything to stop the war in Vietnam."

"Failure to put notice on newspaper that what was contained therein was not official Navy policy."

No one who read Priest's newspaper could have mistaken his views for those of the Navy brass.

Roger Priest may be an old man before he gets out of jail. But he remains defiant. He is not about to bow and scrape in the hope that the brass will show mercy. "These bastards can't be allowed to silence me or any other antiwar serviceman. Keep it up, brass. We'll dance over your graves," Priest has said.

But nothing, *nothing,* more dramatically demonstrates the callousness of the brass than the San Francisco Presidio mutiny trials. Many other anti-war groups played an even greater role than the ASU in bringing those barbarities to the attention of the American people.

The trouble started on October 11, 1968, at the San Francisco Presidio stockade. Private Richard Bunch was five feet, four inches tall, nineteen years old and, among many other things, was described as "manic depressive" by Army psychiatrists. Bunch was convinced that he had been reincarnated twice and that he could walk through walls. Naturally the Army figured the logical place for a man like this was the stockade. On October 11, Bunch made a break for freedom and was killed with a blast in the back from a

12-gauge shotgun. The guard, whom the Army has refused to identify to this day, never called "Halt," as required, before squeezing the trigger. The same day the Army declared the killing "justifiable homicide."

The next day Captain Lamont, the twenty-five-year-old officer in charge of the stockade, gathered the prisoners together and read them Article 94 of the Uniform Code of Military Justice, the section dealing with mutiny. Lamont said he read Article 94 because he feared a prisoner uprising.

Several prisoners who had witnessed Bunch's murder asked permission to give press interviews to counter the Army's "justifiable homicide" verdict. Their requests were denied.

On October 14 the prisoners were assembled for roll call and work-detail assignments at 7:30 A.M. When the first name was called they answered "Here" in unison, walked over to a grassy corner in the stockade enclosure and sat down. When Captain Lamont arrived, one of the men, Walter Pawlowski, stood up and read a list of grievances, including the killing of Private Bunch. Pawlowski also made several requests: the elimination of shotgun-type work details, psychological evaluation of stockade guards and better sanitary conditions. Lamont again began to read Article 94 but was drowned out as the prisoners sang "We Shall Overcome" and "America the Beautiful." Lamont then went to the stockade gate and used a loudspeaker to read Article 94. When the prisoners still refused to move, Lamont called in MPs and fire equipment and ordered water thrown on the demonstrators. The men manning the fire equipment refused to obey him. The MPs then carried the demonstrators back into the stockade barracks. The entire episode lasted one hour and was wholly nonviolent. Twenty-seven prisoners took part in the sit-down. Twenty-six were in the stockade for going AWOL in protest of the war, one was in for punching a sergeant.

On October 22, 1968, Captain Robert L. Paine, who had conducted the preliminary investigation, recommended that the twenty-seven be court-martialed for mutiny. The base legal office prepared the charges the next day.

Private Nesery Sood, twenty-five, married and the father of three children, was the first to be tried. He was found guilty of mutiny, sentenced to fifteen years at hard labor and given a dishonorable discharge with forfeiture of all pay and allowances.

The American Servicemen's Union had been telling everyone who would listen, and a few who didn't care to, about what the Army was doing with the Presidio demonstrators. I had gone to Seattle and led 350 servicemen from Fort Lewis and McCord Air Force Base in a demonstration against the courts-martial. Then I went to San Francisco, where I consulted with some of the movement leaders, who mapped out the massive demonstrations that were to turn the Presidio into a beseiged fortress in the coming weeks.

After that I went out of the country to see two of the accused mutineers, Walter Pawlowski and Keith Mather, who had made a daring Christmas Eve escape from the Presidio stockade and gone into exile. At our meeting I pledged the union's assistance.

Lawrence Reidel and Louis Osczpinski were the next two GIs brought to trial. At their courts-martial Army psychiatrists testified that both men had "serious psychiatric disorders" and should be given administrative discharges. Reidel was given fourteen years, Osczpinski sixteen years.

Now the public was up in arms. Fourteen-, fifteen- and sixteen-year sentences for participating in a sit-down demonstration? Even the press became aroused. Demonstrations demanding that mutiny charges be dropped were held in

116 cities. But this didn't stop the brass. They forged ahead.

Privates Dodd, Yost, Zaino, Murphy, Hayes and Swanson were the next to be tried. Dodd was sentenced to six years at hard labor. Yost, who had his Purple Heart ripped off his uniform on the orders of the prosecution because "he wasn't fit to wear it," was given nine months at hard labor. After suffering a nervous collapse Zaino had his trial postponed pending a sanity hearing. Murphy's trial was also delayed so he could recover from hepatitis. Hayes and Swanson were each sentenced to three years at hard labor. And all because they had sat down for one hour to protest the murder of a fellow GI. The following is the sworn statement of Private Linden Blake, who witnessed the killing:

On Friday, October 11, I was assigned to a work detail with Richard Bunch. We were to go to the hospital and put together wall lockers. Before starting work we went to get a drink of water. I then noticed that Richard Bunch was bothering a guard, asking questions like "Would you shoot me if I ran?" As we started back toward the hospital, I heard Bunch say "Aim for my head," or "You'd better shoot to kill." I wasn't paying very close attention. I had already said something to Bunch like "Don't bug him, he's got a gun." Bunch and the guard were in the middle of the street, two other members of the detail, Colip and Reims, were in the supply room, and I was on the sidewalk, with my back to Bunch and the guard. I heard footsteps, and the click of the shotgun being cocked, and I turned and saw the guard aim and fire, hitting Bunch in the small of the back. The guard gave no command of "Halt" and Bunch was twenty-five to thirty feet from the guard when he was shot. There was one shot fired. After shooting Bunch, the guard whirled, pointed his gun at me and yelled "Hit the ground, hit the ground or I'll shoot you too." Then he seemed to have flipped and said, "I hit him right where I aimed, in the lower back," and then, "Why did I do that? I didn't want to kill anybody, I should have let him go, I didn't want to kill anybody." There were four other witnesses, two were on the detail and saw at least part of what happened, and there were two others who were down the street at the Quartermaster laundry.

The brass had commissioned Captain Richard J. Millard of the United States Army Quartermaster Corps to conduct a pretrial investigation into the courts-martial of Privates Dodd, Yost, Zaino, Murphy, Hayes and Swanson. I have a copy of the recommendations he made. They were almost identical in each case. Here's what Captain Millard said about the Zaino court-martial:

> The charge of mutiny under Article 94 does not apply to the facts of 14 October 1968. There are three elements to the offense of mutiny, one of which is the intent to override lawful military authority. This element is absent in the present case.
>
> I find, however, there are facts sufficient to sustain a charge of willful disobedience under Article 90 of the UCMJ, a lesser included offense of mutiny under Article 94.
>
> In my opinion, this case has been built up out of all proportion. To charge Zaino and the others with mutiny, an offense which has its roots in the harsh admiralty laws of previous centuries, for demonstrating against the conditions that existed in the stockade is, in my opinion, an overreaction by the Army and a misapplication of a statute which could lead to a further miscarriage of justice.
>
> Zaino and the others demonstrated in a manner contrary to military regulations and custom, and they refused to obey the lawful order of Captain Lamont to cease demonstrating and return to the stockade building. For this refusal to obey, I recommend that Private Lawrence J. Zaino be tried by Special Court-martial or as an alternative that he be separated from the service with less than an honorable discharge under AR 635-212.
>
> The two basic reasons for the imposition of punishment are to deter crime and to rehabilitate offenders. In Zaino's case, it is very questionable whether any long-term confinement is likely to be effective in rehabilitating him. I call your attention to the psychiatric evaluation (Incl. 31) prepared by Major Chamberlain at Letterman General Hospital on 18 November 1968. Dr. Chamberlain feels that Private Lawrence J. Zaino has a

personality disorder which makes it highly unlikely that he will be able to adapt to the Army, and therefore recommends that he be separated from the Armed Services as expeditiously as possible under AR 635-212. As far as deterrent to crime is concerned, I feel that a six-month sentence, which is the maximum a Special Court-martial could adjudge, is an adequate deterrent against demonstrations such as the one that occurred on 14 October 1968. If it is not adequate, then the focus of the command should be on those conditions which lead to such demonstrations for, in my opinion, one does not give up six months freedom to participate in a short demonstration unless the conditions leading to the demonstration are compelling.

There is ample testimony in this case to show that the conditions in the stockade prior to 14 October were not up to the standards we should expect. Of special significance in this case is the fact that the DD 510 procedure (allowing prisoners to air grievances), prior to the demonstration on Monday the 14th of October, was shoddy and inefficient. Although the conditions at the stockade were deficient, I do not believe that they were so terrible, or that the prisoners' opportunity to express themselves was so limited, as to be a complete defense to a disobedience of orders. However, these factors should be considered as mitigating circumstances.

Considering all the facts, including the nature of the disturbance, the conditions which existed in the stockade, the military service of the accused, the mental state and character behavior of the accused as described by Dr. Chamberlain, and the unlikelihood that punishment will have any rehabilitative effect, and the established policy that General Court-martial will be reserved for charges that can be disposed of in no other manner consistent with military discipline, I recommend trial by Special Court-martial or, as an alternative, separation under AR 635-212, which would be to the benefit of both the Army and the accused.

Captain Millard's report, commissioned by the Army, went to the following brass hats: Colonel McMahon, Post Commander; Colonel James Garrett, Sixth Army Legal Office; and Lieutenant General Stanley Larsen, Commanding General of the Sixth Army. All three rejected Captain

Millard's recommendations and ordered Lawrence Zaino tried by general court-martial.

With GI restlessness and civilian ire building to a bursting point over the inhuman sentences, did the brass back down? No. Instead the Department of the Army issued a statement proving the brass weren't unmerciful at all: "Although Article 94 of the Uniform Code of Military Justice provides that a person found guilty of mutiny may be punished by death, the Commanding General has referred each case for trial as non-capital, and it will not be possible for the courts-martial to adjudge a death penalty."

CHAPTER XVI   Dozens of left-wing groups are headquartered in New York City. The American Servicemen's Union has a close, cordial and mutually beneficial relationship with a number of these organizations. For example, Students for a Democratic Society, with seventy thousand members throughout the country, channel many of their conscripted adherents into the ASU, and we recommend that ex-GIs about to enter college consider SDS.

Of course, one thing most left-wing organizations have in common is harassment from the FBI. J. Edgar's political police are constantly on the snoop, trailing people, wiretapping phones, breaking into apartments and getting people fired from their jobs.

It has been estimated, probably conservatively, that there are wiretaps on more than 20,000 phones in New York City alone. The Justice Department has admitted that Martin Luther King's phone was tapped. So was heavyweight champion Muhammed Ali's. When the Government set out to jail Jimmy Hoffa, head of the teamsters' union, wiretapping was only one of many methods it used.

Supposedly, most of the information the FBI gathers by wiretapping can't be used against anyone. J. Edgar Hoover, however, has found a way to get around this inconvenience.

His agents merely leak the information they have learned to the press, who then proceed to try the man in print. A questioner wrote to *Parade,* the Sunday supplement magazine, and asked if the wiretap on Martin Luther King's phone had provided evidence linking him to the Communist party. No, said *Parade,* which then proceeded to libel Dr. King by saying that the wiretap had proved that he had a rather "lively" sex life. Guess who fed that lie to *Parade?* And guess who was dead and couldn't defend himself?

Represented by the American Civil Liberties Union, the ASU has joined with eleven other organizations, and filed suit against J. Edgar Hoover to have the wiretaps taken off our phones. Even if we win, however, we do not expect Hoover to abide by the court's ruling, because J. Edgar Hoover is the law. But we can't allow ourselves to be intimidated. Too often in the past, movements have been paralyzed by fear of repression. Yet it is a fact that no mass movement has ever been crushed by police surveillance and infiltration.

Nevertheless the FBI keeps trying. After 477 air-traffic controllers called in sick in June 1969 to protest conditions caused by the greed of airlines that would land a plane every three seconds if they could get away with it, the FBI installed wiretaps on their union's phone. The Professional Air Traffic Controllers Organization charged the FBI with "union busting."

Indeed, the FBI has never been fond of unions. Hand in hand with the brass, they have striven mightily to put the American Servicemen's Union out of business. But the ASU is needed; ask any GI, visit any Army base, try to live on an enlisted man's pay, count the coffins being taken off airplanes returned from Vietnam. No governmental pressure can stop an idea whose time has come.

Lest anyone think the brass are merely against a union

for GIs, let's examine the Army's inglorious record of intervention on the side of big business against the unions.

In 1877, workers on the Pennsylvania Railroad struck for a wage that would at least permit their families to eat. Tom Scott, president of the Pennsylvania Railroad, said, "Give the strikers a rifle diet for a few days and see how they like that kind of bread." President Rutherford Hayes obliged by dispatching troops to Illinois, New Mexico, Colorado, Missouri, Maryland and Pennsylvania; and when the strike had been crushed, thirty-two workers were killed and hundreds were wounded.

Andrew Carnegie couldn't be accused of generosity to his workers, but, like his more sophisticated modern counterparts, was never miserly when it came to handouts to top Government officials. So when workers went on strike in 1892 at his Homestead, Pennsylvania, steel plant, it was only right that his favors be returned. Eight thousand soldiers broke up the strike, and the union leaders were indicted for treason.

Not much has changed. Scores of ASU organizers languish behind barbed wire because they dared suggest that GIs have rights, dared stand up to their bosses and say, "We don't like this deal!" And for every soldier who has fallen in this just fight, ten have risen to take his place. History is on our side.

In 1903, miners at Cripple Creek, Colorado, went on strike to protest slave wages and dangerous working conditions. Once again the Army was called to protect the interests of a millionaire, in this case John D. Rockefeller, who owned the mines. Strike leaders were jailed, and when a union lawyer presented General Sherman Bell with a writ of habeas corpus, Bell replied, *"Habeas corpus,* hell! We'll give them *post mortems!"* But this strike would not easily be broken. Conditions in the mines were inhuman—cave-ins and pit-gas poisonings were commonplace—and wages were whatever the boss wanted to pay. One newspaper editor lambasted General Bell, and Bell threw him and his entire staff into a stockade. Still it wasn't over. Hundreds of striking workers were loaded onto freight cars and sent to detention camps. The final count was 42 workers killed, 112 wounded and 1,345 arrested.

And John D. Rockefeller got richer. He got richer for the same reasons corporations grow fat today with foreign investments: the United States Army is there to protect them. Just as it was the GI who did the dirty work for the rich at Cripple Creek in 1903, so it is the GI who is forced to fight and die in the sweltering jungles of Vietnam.

The Army has been good to General Motors. In 1936 more than one hundred thousand GM employees began a strike at Flint, Michigan, by sitting down inside the plants. However, the duPont-controlled GM had gotten wind of the upcoming strike and had obtained the assistance of Army and Navy Intelligence agents, who set about busily to uncover the names of union organizers so they could be fired. Despite their efforts the strike got under way, and General Motors went to court. Judge Edward D. Black (he owned $219,000 of GM stock) ripped off an injunction ordering the workers to vacate the plants within twenty-four hours. The workers ignored the injunction and the Army moved in with 37-mm howitzers. But this time the strikers won, because they wouldn't be pushed any more and because General Motors was afraid of the damage (not the lives that would be lost, but the damage) that would be done to their plants if the Army used the howitzers. The courageous men who refused to move even though they might have been annihilated are those responsible for the unionization of the auto industry.

It is easy to understand why the brass are congenitally

incapable of accepting the American Servicemen's Union. When we succeed, they will no longer be able to command mindless obedience and unassailable privilege.

June 1941 saw crack infantrymen, described by the New York *Daily News* as "bronzed veterans recently returned from long service in the Orient," called out to crush a strike at North American Aviation, and once again it was the Army versus the People. Equipped with antiaircraft guns, antitank guns, trench mortars and rifles, the soldiers routed the workers from their picket lines, and Inglewood, California, was placed under martial law. Why were the workers striking? Because they wanted their pay raised from forty cents an hour to seventy-five cents an hour. J. H. Kindleberger, president of North American Aviation, said, "I don't have to pay any more to my workers because most of them are young kids who spend their money on a flivver and a gal."

To avert a nationwide strike of railroad workers in 1950, Commander-in-Chief Truman put a million railroad employees under military control and gave seven railroad magnates military authority. Six of them didn't even have to be commissioned; they were recalled to "active duty" as Colonels. In effect, President Truman's order fully protected the railroad owners' profits but forbade any changes in wages, hours and working conditions except by consent of the corporations.

In October 1955 the Army used four Sherman tanks to crush a strike at the Perfect Circle Corporation in New Castle, Indiana. Nine workers were injured in what the *Wall Street Journal* described as "Perfect Circle's fight for the workers' right to hold a job without belonging to a union."

The brass have become more sophisticated in the 1960s. They have discovered that naked force is not always necessary when intervening against strikers. The following is a letter the ASU received from the United Farm Workers, AFL-CIO, who are leading the California grape strike:

"Enclosed are figures relating to the grape strike and to the Department of Defense purchase of grapes, which show how military buying of scab grapes has escalated dramatically. Is this Department of Defense buying a result of 'a high troop acceptability factor' or 'a craving for grapes,' as Pentagon officials say?"

What has happened is that the Army's purchase of grapes has risen 400 percent since the strike began.

The brass have strange notions about why strikes occur. Here's the way they put it in the handbook *Democracy vs. Communism:* "Communists also try to start strikes, knowing that long drawn out strikes bring misery to the workers and their families. A carefully trained Communist agent tries to capture control of a whole plant or shop by getting himself elected shop steward. Then he can cook up grievances, stir up discontent and pave the way for a strike." The handbook goes on to describe the strikes "Stalin ordered in the United States."

GIs don't always buy the Army's explanation for worker discontent. The first troops sent into Pittsburgh in 1877 to crush a railroad strike threw down their weapons and joined the strikers. Many enlisted men wore union buttons on their uniforms during the 1936 strike at General Motors, and three years earlier many GIs went AWOL rather than smash picket lines at the Autolite plant in Toledo, Ohio.

GIs have occasionally stood up to the brass alone. During the Homestead strike in 1892 an enlisted man named William Iams let out a cheer when it was announced that Henry Frick, chairman of Carnegie Steel, had been shot by a worker. Unfortunately the cheer was overheard by Lieutenant Colonel J. B. Streator, who demanded an apology. Iams refused and was hung by the thumbs until he passed out.

But the brass never did get an apology out of him, nor did Henry Frick, who was only slightly wounded, apologize to the dozens of workers who were injured.

Walter Trumbull was another GI who chose to side with labor instead of management. The year was 1929 and Trumbull was among hundreds of enlisted men sent to put down a strike of sugar-plantation workers in Hawaii. For urging his fellow GIs to support the workers Trumbull was sentenced to twenty-six years in Alcatraz. Incidentally, Walter Trumbull was the only person, until the ASU came into being, to advocate a union for GIs, and his demands were similar to those of the American Servicemen's Union.

Entire books have been written showing how the brass have always sided with the rich. The reason is clear: those who run the Army are bosses, too, and anything that increases the power of those under them decreases their own.

CHAPTER XVII   In January 1969 the American Servicemen's Union had forty-five hundred card-carrying members and was receiving so many requests for help from AWOL or court-martialed GIs that we started keeping our office open from 9 A.M. to 10:30 P.M., six days a week. Dick Wheaton and I addressed student groups, appeared on radio and television talk shows and conducted fund-raising drives among civilians. The union's expenses were high. Rare was the day we didn't receive collect long-distance calls from California, Hawaii or Sweden. But the lawyers were great. If we couldn't pay their fee they often worked for nothing.

On college campuses we hit hard at the brass. We quoted Nguyen Cao Ky (June 1965): "I have only one idol, Adolph Hitler. We need four or five Hitlers in Vietnam." And we quoted Lyndon Johnson (February 1966): "I hope that young Americans will show the same fanaticism fighting for our system as young Nazis showed during World War II." At a number of universities the ASU was able to spark campaigns to kick ROTC, the officer factory, off campus.

The brass were vulnerable on a thousand issues: for instance, the Army's DD 98 form, which lists "disloyal" organizations. One looks in vain for the American Nazi party or the John Birch Society but easily finds the Jewish Cultural Society, the Jewish People's Committee, the Jewish People's Fraternal Order, the American Jewish Labor Council and the School of Jewish Studies. Hitler couldn't have drawn up a more fascistic document.

Also interesting to students we talked to was United States Army Artillery and Missile Command Regulation 28-86, which is a recommended reading list for officers. It includes *Panzer Leader,* written by Heinz Guderian, the notorious Nazi General who headed Hitler's general staff. Guderian presided over the military "Court of Honor" that handed tens of thousands of antifascist German soldiers over to the hangman. Guderian's crimes are reported without remorse in *Panzer Leader.* Twenty-five years ago his name was near the top of the list of America's worst enemies. Today his book is recommended reading for officers.

But former Nazi officers often manage to escape punishment. General Graf von Kielmansegg was one of the engineers of Hitler's death machine and he enjoyed his work. He wrote a book, *Tanks Between Warsaw and the Atlantic,* which hailed his exploits for Der Führer. Guess what happened to General von Kielmansegg? Today he is the commander of all NATO forces in Central Europe, and has direct authority over 200,000 American and British GIs.

Graf von Kielmansegg is small potatoes alongside West German Chancellor Kurt Kiesinger, a former Nazi propaganda chief, and President Heinrich Lubke, who helped build the slave-labor camps where Hitler sent his enemies to die.

The brass never blink when they send poor blacks and poor whites to die in Vietnam. But how about the rich? How many Rockefellers and duPonts have been killed in the war? How many Mellons and Whitneys and Firestones? Not many. They're too busy learning how to run Daddy's financial empire, so that if a GI survives in Vietnam he can come home to work and make money for them. ˗

Probably owing to a bureaucratic blunder, Robert Flaherty, the son of a large war materials manufacturer, was actually inducted into the Armed Forces. He was stationed with some of our ASU members at El Centro, a naval air base in Southern California. There his money bought him off having to do regular work like an ordinary GI. He had his own airplane and, even though it was illegal, was allowed to fly it onto the base airfield. He lounged around from Monday through Thursday and each Friday was given the day off so he could fly back to Los Angeles for a three-day weekend.

The two years of oppression experienced by a white GI gives him some hint of what black and brown people in America face their entire lives. The ASU believes that black servicemen, being the most oppressed, will play the most militant and advanced role in the struggle. Our recognition of this has won us allies among many of the organizations that represent oppressed national minorities within the United States. The Student National Coordinating Committee (SNCC), the Pro-Independence Movement of Puerto Rico (MPI), the Nation of Islam and the Black Panther party have all expressed support for the work of the ASU.

Perhaps the viewpoint of Afro-American servicemen is best expressed in *Listen, Brother!*, a pamphlet the ASU has distributed throughout the Armed Forces. Its author, Robert Williams, was forced into exile after he organized a self-defense group in Monroe, North Carolina, to protect against Klan violence. A former marine sergeant, Williams makes a passionate plea to black GIs not to fight against the Vietnamese:

Deadly planes, loaded with rockets and napalm, zoom through the sky. The hunt, the pogrom is on. The screaming eagles of death are vicious, like mad dogs, in their crazed desire to burn, maim and kill the colored flesh of the hard-fighting and hard-working Vietnamese. The inevitable command comes down from the big white father to go in pursuit and search of the fighting Vietnamese. Remotely, and almost in a daze, you amble like a grizzly bear out of your cave of hibernation. Like an obedient dog you go in search of a people fighting to drive invaders from their land. The word is to kill all, burn all, destroy all. What a horrible thing to do to poor colored people with such meager belongings. You stumble into the valley. You feel sick and numb inside. You can smell the stench of burnt flesh, of dead and decaying bodies. You see the human carnage of women and children, of old men. How colored they look with their dead eyes frozen in a final moment of petrifying horror and terror. You get an alert signal. The vicious enemy is being flushed from a rickety bamboo shack. A monstrous tank rumbles into position and levels its deadly guns to cover the captives now being flushed out with tear gas. Rocket launchers and machine guns are aimed. A frightened but defiant child emerges. Deep and pain-racked groans filter from the shack. The defiant child points angrily at the shack. How colored this child is. How poor he is. Finally, with the child in front as a shield, the "guardians of democracy" advance into the shack. The prey has been captured. An old granny, with her back raw from napalm, her eyes burnt out, is "another Vietcong apprehended by the American forces."

Now listen, brother, where is your conscience?

Brother, being a black man in the racist white man's world is a hurting thing. To live with yourself, to keep cool, you have to alibi the man to your own heart and the more you alibi for him against your own best interest, the more he is convinced that you are a natural brainless fool. It's a vicious circle. Well, anyway, you keep telling yourself like all of the black veterans before you that things will be better after the war, that you are earning your rights the hard way, and that you ain't gonna take no more of that white man's shit when you get back home. Brother, who is kidding whom? Now let's lay it on the line and

> tell it like it is. How in the hell can you let Mr. Charlie bring you 10,000 miles from home to bring white man's justice to colored Vietnam NOW, to fight and die NOW in instant action in Vietnam while your freedom has been deferred for 400 years and the man is still deferring and stalling? Brother, why is the black man's freedom always in the future and everybody else's is now? Listen, Brother, you aren't going to be any freer tomorrow than you were yesterday.

There's a revolt in the Army, and the brass know it. The desertion rate has doubled in 1969, which means that more than 380,000 GIs will desert rather than go to Vietnam in the next two years if the war continues. Many of these men will go to Canada, where the people speak English and where there are some jobs. Others will go to Sweden, Japan, Great Britain and France. Most will be in hiding right here in the United States.

But what really worries the brass is that for the last year the desertion rate of GIs in Vietnam has stood at ten a day. Because of a war they neither want nor believe in, many of these soldiers have defected to the National Liberation Front for sanctuary. The brass doesn't like to talk about this, it's bad for morale, but the fact remains that hundreds of GIs have voluntarily gone over to the other side. In July 1969 the New York *Post* reported that the Army had admitted sending out Green Berets to capture or kill defected American servicemen. When asked to describe the function of the Green Berets, Major A. Lincoln German, the training director of the Green Beret Special Warfare School at Fort Bragg, North Carolina, had this to say: "We're a kind of Peace Corps."

An article in the July 14, 1967, *New York Times* sheds light on why GIs are fed up. At Con Thien the Third Marine Division had been under heavy shelling for weeks and the men were close to rebellion. A *Times* reporter interviewed their Commanding General about it. The interview took place at his headquarters, sixty miles behind the action. Here's what the General said: "Hell, you give them a kick in the butt and shake them up a little and they'll be all right."

Another sixty-miles-behind-the-lines hero, a major, chimed in: "All we need is a little shoot-em-up action and we'll be okay."

It's hard to top that for bravery. And when his men got clobbered, don't think he didn't get a medal for bravery.

Another *New York Times* reporter, Bernard Weinraub, wrote about a briefing session he had attended in 1968. "Well," said a Brigadier General, "I'm happy to say that the Army's casualties finally caught up with the Marines' last week."

"You don't mean you're happy," said an astonished listener.

"The Army should be doing their job, too," replied the General.

The brass like to award each other medals. Captain William Carpenter was decorated for bravery after calling for napalm strikes that killed sixteen GIs and burned many more. *Newsweek* echoed the brass when it wrote: "Who can forget the courage of Captain William Carpenter, the famous 'lonely end' at West Point and a former All-American? Badly outnumbered and on the verge of being overrun by a North Vietnamese unit in the central highlands, Carpenter called in an air strike on his own position."

"I lost a lot of people in that strike," Carpenter said.

He lost a lot? What about the GIs who were killed or horribly burned? Carpenter wasn't even hurt.

At any rate, Carpenter's sadness was probably dispelled by the medals he received and the soft position he was assigned to afterward.

We all remember when the assault on Hamburger Hill resulted in more than three hundred dead GIs. Then, when the hill was finally taken, the brass ordered the GIs to abandon it. The NLF promptly moved back up and a General said: "I'm prepared to go up and take it again."

Sometimes, however, the men strike back. *GI Says,* a mimeographed underground sheet put out by the guys in the 101st Airborne Division, called for the death of Lieutenant Colonel Weldon Honeycutt, the much-decorated field commander who had repeatedly ordered his men up Hamburger Hill. *GI Says* offered a reward of $10,000 for Honeycutt's neck. One attempt to collect the money was made by a soldier who booby-trapped Honeycutt's quarters with grenades and claymore mines.

But it is the arbitrary use of courts-martial, which the brass employ to keep GIs in line, that servicemen most resent. A "crime" in civilian life usually consists of a poor man stealing from a rich man. In the Army it is considered a crime when a GI refuses to accept the fact that he's a lowly turd who has to obey every order his officers give, and the criminal offense usually falls into the following categories:

Saying to hell with it and going AWOL.

Telling an officer to jack off.

Punching an officer in the mouth.

Now, there is nothing morally wrong with any of these things. In fact, they deserve applause from all people who believe in rooting for the underdog. But according to military law (written by the brass), which is akin to the old slave laws, these acts are Federal crimes.

In 1966 there were 67,000 courts-martial. Ninety-five percent of these resulted in guilty verdicts. But even that figure is misleading. Some of those being court-martialed were officers, and fewer than 50 percent of those cases brought guilty findings.

The July 28, 1967, San Francisco *Chronicle* revealed how officers stick together:

Captain Paul C. Ogg of the First Cavalry Division was found not guilty last night of ordering the death of a suspected Vietcong prisoner of war.

An Army general court-martial of six officers cleared the 34-year-old captain of any role in the killing of the Vietnamese peasant in a village on the Bong Son plains on April 4.

Three enlisted men have been tried and convicted of killing the Vietnamese. All three—and several other enlisted men— testified that they heard a radio conversation in which Ogg had told a platoon leader to kill the prisoner.

Outside the courtroom, Ogg chatted with his attorney, Captain Eugene W. Murphy of LaCrosse, Wisconsin. Less than a dozen feet away stood the silent, glaring members of C Company, some of whom had given testimony that they had heard Ogg say by radio of the Vietnamese, "shoot him."

In September 1969 the Permanent Subcommittee on Investigations of the U.S. Senate began hearings on the activities of Major General Carl C. Turner and First Sergeant Major of the Army William O. Wooldridge. It was alleged that they were part of a military Mafia that had been stealing millions of dollars of enlisted men's money from service clubs. Wooldridge had also been smuggling tax-free liquor back to the States from Vietnam in General Creighton Abrams' private plane. So far the only punishment meted out has been an order rescinding Wooldridge's Distinguished Service Medal. The GI who served six months in the Long Binh stockade for stealing a peanut butter sandwich must have been greatly impressed by this further demonstration of "military justice."

Turner, who on retirement was appointed by Nixon to head the entire Federal Marshal system, stated a short time before his exposure, "The cause of all the immorality in America today is that young people don't stand up straight and salute the flag any more."

Also mentioned in the Senate hearings but unpunished were Major General William A. Cunningham, III, who was accused of pigeonholding an investigation of Wooldridge and Brigadier General Earl F. Cole, whose connections with the head of a Hong Kong firm called Sarl Electronics implicated him in the scandal.

According to the September 12, 1967, Staten Island *Advance,* more than half a million men carry the brand of an undesirable discharge. In civilian life these half-million men are virtually blacklisted. Because of an arbitrary act that is a violation of the most basic guarantees of the Constitution, they are made second-class citizens, which means, among many other things, that they are deprived of the right to certain jobs.

Again, according to the Staten Island *Advance,* "In one hundred percent of all discharge cases, he [the defendant] has no right to examine the evidence against him, no right to confront his accusers, to subpoena witnesses on his own behalf or to have a record of his hearing."

On July 15, 1968, the American Servicemen's Union wrote to the State Department and demanded that they apologize to North Korea for the Pueblo incident so that the crew could be released. Deputy Assistant Secretary of State G. McMurtrie Godley answered by saying that to apologize would "amount to asserting that our statements to date regarding the Pueblo have been false."

Almost a year after the spy ship was captured the United States finally did apologize, and the crew was released. And when the ASU demanded the right to be present at the Pueblo inquiry, Admiral T. H. Moorer, Chief of Naval Operations, refused to allow us to be a party of interest. But each day the union membership grows, and the day is coming when the likes of Moorer will be forced to act on our demands.

In exposing the separate and unequal care afforded

wounded GIs at Walter Reed Hospital, the late Drew Pearson gave one excellent reason why GIs need a union. "There was only one shower," Pearson wrote, "and four wash basins for all the men in the ward. Forty-five beds were crowded into one room. Young men, arms and legs blown off in Vietnam, hobble and jostle around the packed quarters."

But downstairs in the officers' hospital quarters, Pearson learned, everybody had a separate room that was clean and pleasant and cooled by an air-conditioner.

Walter Reed is not an isolated example. The ASU receives letters every day complaining about filthy conditions and absurd rules. At Tripler Army Hospital in Honolulu, Hawaii, wounded men were forced to *lie* at attention whenever an officer entered the room.

In 1959 and 1960 a House of Representatives committee revealed some interesting facts about where the true loyalties of the brass reside:

Boeing Aircraft, the number-one supplier of war goods, had 61 retired officers on its payroll. Five of these were flag rank or General.

General Dynamics was the number-two war-goods supplier and, as number twos ought, was trying harder: it had 186 retired officers, 27 of whom were flag rank or Generals.

Lockheed Aircraft had 171 retired brass hats; again, 27 of these were Generals or of comparable rank.

The point is obvious. The brass-brains are business partners of the largest corporations in the world. War is not hell to the brass; it's the big payoff.

General MacArthur went to work for Remington-Rand at $100,000 a year. Continental Can gave General Lucius Clay $108,000 a year. Lesser Generals have it tougher. They only receive $75,000 a year. In 1969, Congressional hearings chaired by Senator Proxmire disclosed that more than two thousand former high-ranking Army officers are now employed by war industries.

Most GIs are aware of the shuttle service between the Pentagon and the large defense contractors. *All* GIs know about the recently voted across-the-board pay increases. A private now earns $1,428 a year—after taxes, about $98 a month. The Joint Chiefs of Staff now make $50,000. Best of all, Commander in Chief Nixon's pay was boosted from $100,000 to $200,000 a year.

CHAPTER XVIII   By July 1969 the American Servicemen's Union had sixty-five hundred members. In one sense this was a disappointment; it made us seem like a small group that the brass could wave away as unimportant. After all, an outfit that can dismiss a quarter of a million Pentagon marchers as insignificant surely wasn't going to admit that they were impressed by a sixty-five-hundred-member union. Yet we knew our support among GIs was much broader than our membership figures indicated. The brass knew it, too, and they weren't going to accept it lying down. Employing a variety of repressive measures, they were doing their best to curtail our activities.

There are congressmen, however, who don't think the brass have been tough enough against the antiwar movement.

At a hearing before a subcommittee of the Committee on Appropriations in the House of Representatives in March 1969, none other than the chief of Intelligence, Brigadier General Vasco J. Fenili, was grilled by certain congressmen. This General, whose agents report to him from every country in the world and who is accustomed to do the questioning himself, had to provide answers as to why he hadn't been able to prevent organized disaffection in his own back yard.

Representative Robert L. Sikes of Florida and Representative Glenard P. Lipscomb of California asked some pointed questions about me and the American Servicemen's Union. The General was assisted in his answers by a Mr. Braunstein, whom he introduced as "a retired lieutenant colonel, in counterintelligence work."

Following are excerpts from the published hearing:

MR. SIKES: Of course, it is obvious that not everyone in uniform is happy with the service or happy about being in uniform. A certain amount of that is inevitable . . .

MR. BRAUNSTEIN: . . . As the war progressed we found that there were more deliberate instances of dissidence . . . One individual in this category that made considerable headlines was an individual by the name of Andrew Stapp.

MR. LIPSCOMB: You say that in the past tense.

MR. BRAUNSTEIN: Right. He is no longer in the service.

MR. LIPSCOMB: Right. But he is very active now.

MR. BRAUNSTEIN: Right; he is. He is the father, so to speak, of the American Servicemen's Union, so-called, which purports to be attempting to unionize the Army.

MR. LIPSCOMB: He also publishes a paper entitled *The Bond*.

MR. BRAUNSTEIN: He publishes *The Bond*.

MR. LIPSCOMB: Both of you gentlemen have tapped this subject very lightly up to this moment, I think. I mean, you have left the impression that it is no problem—or have I been wrong?

GENERAL FENILI: Well, we know there are 14 of such newspapers. We do know there are these various organizations . . . It is always a threat, sir, but we don't feel that it is a major threat at this particular time . . .

MR. LIPSCOMB: But I do not think, as intelligence officers,

you should leave this committee with the idea that this paper is no problem . . . the fact is that the newspapers in Moscow continually publish material from these papers on both Moscow radio and newspapers. You mentioned here there was no Communist link. Mr. Stapp was in the press, in the *Wall Street Journal,* just a week ago criticizing *The Green Beret,* a motion picture. . . . Mr. Stapp was in the military with two other fellows and it all started there while you observed him getting started, I suppose. But if it can be done once, it certainly can be done again. . . . I recognize the right of free speech and individual privileges, but at the same time I recognize it can endanger the security of our country.

MR. BRAUNSTEIN: Yes, sir. We are well aware of that.

MR. LIPSCOMB: So actually from just observing it from the outside, from public notices and what I can gather, it seems to be growing in magnitude and not reducing in its significance.

The brass also strenuously sought out reasons to court-martial union members, assigning them the most dangerous jobs in the Army, even classifying the union as a "subversive" group. By these fear tactics the brass warned away prospective members. Better, some GIs think, to suffer it out in silence than to risk the ire of the Army and all the social repercussions that can carry. The brass are expert practitioners in the use of fear, and fear, in large, unremitting doses, can often discourage effective dissent.

Fear of the brass is something very different from fear of battle. Throughout history rulers have been able to persuade people to overcome their fear of battle and war while at the same time imbuing the general population with a terrible dread of going against custom and facing social opprobrium.

So in one sense the American Servicemen's Union was

hampered by the brass. But in another we found real cause to be heartened by the figure of sixty-five hundred. The union was just a little more than a year old. It advocated ideas so radical, so different from the general canon that they were bound to take time before they found wide acceptance. And our membership was constantly growing. More and more young people, having been exposed to new ideas and not willing to rubber-stamp the established order, were coming of draft age. Many of these young people were students who had been fighting on campus against the ruthlessness of intransigent authority. Others were militant youth from the ghettos, youth not willing to take "Later" for an answer when they demanded their rights. So we were full of confidence for the future. We had a ready-made, ever-growing, never-ending supply of men and women whose very nature would turn away in revulsion from the military and what it stands for.

But the American Servicemen's Union was also strong in the men it already had, the dedicated realists who had come with us in the early stages of the fight. These were not shaky friends or thrill-seeking adventurers, people who were just joiners by nature. They had known what they were getting into and had risked harassment and reprisals to do it.

We all understood that ours was a long-range goal, something that would not be realized in a year or two of part-time effort but that could, given time and persistence, shake the very foundations of American society.

The ASU has encouraged a number of pro-union GIs to put out their own papers simply because they are more familiar with conditions on their own bases than we at the national headquarters are. Altogether, ASU members are involved in putting out newspapers at ten different bases, and in Keflavik, Iceland, union members have their own radio transmitter. The brass would love to put it out of operation but can't find it. The GIs keep moving it from place to place, always one jump ahead of the brass.

The underground newspapers put out at military installations set GIs to talking—and to thinking. They may start off by thinking of the inequality of the enlisted men's quarters and pay compared to that of the officers. They may start by becoming angry at having to treat officers like gods. They may start by comparing the rotten jobs they have to the easy work the sergeants do. Worse, they may find themselves asking why this country unhesitatingly sends soldiers to 109 countries around the globe and lavishes attention on some of the worst dictatorships this century has been forced to witness, simply because they are anti-Communist.

Again and again the story repeats itself. The United States barges in with rockets rattling, checkbooks in hand, tanks and guns at the ready, to prop up fascist dictatorships or military juntas. Why? Because "we" have investments to protect. The United States has troops in Spain, Greece, South Korea, Portugal, Taiwan, Thailand, Haiti and Ethiopia, to name but a few. In each case the soldiers are there to guard the investments of the likes of Esso, Caltex, United Fruit, Coca-Cola and the Bank of America. For years our rulers fawned over Batista in Cuba, until Castro, shaking the Sierra Maestra with his footfalls, descended on Havana and overthrew the tyrant.

The tragedy is that Americans die, they actually die, because the ruling class and their puppets—the brass—serve their own interests and not those of the people.

The real heroes of history are the masses of people, the scores of thousands who watered the ground with their blood stopping and defeating the Nazis at the gates of Stalingrad, the one million Algerians who died to free their nation, the Vietnamese peasants who stormed the seemingly impregnable French defenses at Dien Bien Phu, the African guerrilla fighters who have liberated huge areas of their homeland from Portuguese colonialism, the Cuban rebels who died before Batista's machine guns at the Moncada Barracks, the Chinese people, one quarter of the human race, rising from one hundred years of Western dominance and enslavement, the black and brown Americans whose rebellions have shaken more than two hundred American cities and, yes, the GIs in the ASU who have been sent to the stockade because they fought for what is right.